SOVIET YOUTH CULTURE

Also by Jim Riordan

SPORT IN SOVIET SOCIETY
SPORT UNDER COMMUNISM: China, Cuba, Czechoslovakia, GDR, USSR
SOVIET UNION: Land and People
EASTERN EUROPE: The Lands and their Peoples
SOVIET EDUCATION: The Gifted and the Handicapped

Soviet Youth Culture

Edited by

Jim Riordan

Professor of Russian Studies
University of Bradford

MACMILLAN

First published 1989

Published by
THE MACMILLAN PRESS LTD
Houndmills, Basingstoke, Hampshire RG21 2XS
and London
Companies and representatives
throughout the world

Typset by Footnote Graphics,
Warminster, Wilts

Printed in China

British Library Cataloguing in Publication Data
Soviet youth culture.
1. Soviet Union. Young persons. Social problems
I. Riordan, James. 1936–
362.7′042′0947
ISBN 0–333–46231–9 (hardcover)
ISBN 0–333–49426–1 (paperback)

20 2 90

Contents

Acknowledgement

The editor would like to express gratitude to the Leverhulme Trust and Bradford University Modern Languages Research Committee for their generous support of this project.

JIM RIORDAN

Notes on the Contributors

The team of contributors consists of Russian-speaking scholars who have all lived and studied in the Soviet Union.

Sue Bridger is Research Fellow in the Modern Languages Centre at the University of Bradford, and author of *Women in the Soviet Countryside* (1987).

Tanya Frisby is Lecturer in Russian Studies at the Institute of Soviet and East European Studies in the University of Glasgow, and one-time Soviet student at Moscow State University.

Paul Easton was recently a student of Russian at Portsmouth Polytechnic; he spent a year in the Soviet rock music community.

Friedrich Kuebart is Senior Lecturer at the Arbeitsstelle für vergleichende Bildungsforschung, Institut für Pädagogik of the University of the Ruhr at Bochum.

Jim Riordan is Professor of Russian Studies at the University of Bradford; he was a youth correspondent and translator for five years in Moscow.

Introduction

In a number of communist states young people have recently emerged as pioneers of change, leading some commentators to draw parallels with the events of the 1960s that shook the West. The young Moscow intellectual Boris Kagarlitsky writes of the similarities in Soviet youth culture today with 'the best examples of Western youth counterculture in the sixties'; and as 'in the West in the sixties, interest has increased sharply in both Marxism and utopian socialism'.[1]

In the 1960s, rebellious youth culture, expressed in music, dress, even soft drugs, proved to be the harbinger of social radicalisation among Western youth, many of whom made the leap from particular grievances to universal transformation, challenging hierarchy, institutional totems of bourgeois culture, gender, discrimination, racial oppression and the colonisation of everyday life by the capitalist state and militarism.

Today it seems to be the turn of youth in countries like the USSR, China, Poland and Bulgaria as they campaign for radical change and democracy. And once again youth culture is the heady medium of expression for protest against the establishment, against corruption and alienation of the personality. Their initiative is not a response to any appeal from on high. In the USSR, for example, independently of the will of the leadership, a new youth movement began to be formed in the early 1980s, well before the advent of Mikhail Gorbachov.

An interesting aspect of Gorbachov's USSR since March 1985, however, is the way the leadership is responding with an openness and determination to reveal a whole range of phenomena that just a couple of years ago it had suppressed. As a young actor in the popular Latvian film about youth problems, *It Isn't Easy to be Young*, has said, 'Youth problems have been around a long time, but they were stifled ... We were protected from knowing too much about ourselves.'[2] Yet today we read quite regularly in Soviet periodicals of punks and hippies, night bikers and drug addicts, soccer hooligans and muggers, glue sniffers and prostitutes (male and female), vigilante gangs and skinheads (known as 'British horrors'), Zen Bhuddists and Hari Krishna followers, even Swastika-sporting young fascists. It is evidently now felt that honesty is the best policy. After all, youth disaffection from official organisations and values is a widespread and growing problem, and is frequently admitted as such.

Youth is not always what it seems. To some Western scholars youth is confined to the teenage years. Soviet writers, however, tend to set broader parameters. Typically, Academician Yakovlev, Secretary of the Party Central Committee, puts 'Soviet youth in the 14–32 age band.'[3] This makes it a sizeable group. Just over ten years ago, in 1977, there were some seventy million people in the 15–30 age group, but with the falling birth rate, the number has declined to sixty-four million in 1987, just under a quarter of the total Soviet population.[4]

As regards the nature of Soviet youth, it is well to remember that their background differs considerably from that of most Western youth. Not only are most Soviet young people at an earlier stage of modernisation and the 'rural-urban continuum' (as many as 40 per cent of young urban workers were born in the countryside), they do not experience unemployment (often said to be a major source of tension, alienation and social ills in the West). On the other hand, they do experience work frustrations and exhibit a high degree of occupational mobility.

Soviet youth is as richly diverse as is youth in any modern society. All young people are not agitating for change in the same direction or at the same pace. In fact, some exhibit symptoms of what Erich Fromm once called 'escape from freedom', seeing in freedom and democracy (or, at least, in *perestroika* and *glasnost*) a threat to set traditions, law and order, and security. Some young people evidently have a nostalgia for Stalinism, what one youth editor has called wishing to 'model their behaviour on the most distressing period of our history'.[5] The Slavophile v Westernisers debate still finds an echo with Soviet youth in the last decades of the twentieth century. We should also remember that a large proportion of disaffected youth is confined to the major urban centres and it has evoked equally strong reaction from others. Any study (especially a Western one) of Soviet youth may therefore be unbalanced through what it excludes – either the rebellious and deviant on the one hand, or the conservative and traditional lifestyles of the 'silent majority' on the other. This imbalance is particularly apposite in such a multi-ethnic, unevenly developed society as the USSR.

The authors do not pretend to have avoided bias, whether through age or social conditioning; but they have attempted to present as broad a canvas as possible of Soviet youth and their problems, from schoolchildren (Kuebart) to farmers (Bridger), from the rock music

community (Easton) to the Komsomol (Riordan), from youth culture
and subculture (Frisby) to conservative reaction (Riordan). And
since it would be arrogant to publish a book on youth written solely
by 'old fogies', we have ensured that contributors range from 'senior
veterans' to a research student and undergraduate. All, though, are
young in heart.

JIM RIORDAN

Notes

1. Kagarlitsky, Boris, 'The intelligentsia and the changes', *New Left
   Review*, July/August 1987, no. 164, pp. 18–19.
2. Matizen, V., 'Ot otchayaniya k nadezhde' ('From despair to hope'),
   Iskusstvo kino, 1987, no. 4, p. 37.
3. Yakovlev, A., *Kontrapropaganda – odna iz sostavnykh chastei sovetskoi
   ideologii (Counter-propaganda – a component part of Soviet ideology)*
   (Moscow: Politizdat, 1983) p. 7.
4. Ilinsky, Igor, 'Perestroika sostitsya yesli. . .' ('*Perestroika* will take place
   if . . .'), *Molodoi kommunist*, 1987, no. 12, p. 15.
5. See Likhanov, A., *Knizhnoye obozrenie*, 1987, no. 9; quoted in Kagarlitsky, p. 22. Likhanov is editor of the youth magazine *Smena* and a
   popular writer of teenage fiction.

1 Soviet Youth Culture
Tanya Frisby

'Let me speak.' 'May I say something?' Young people try to reach
the microphone. Some are unkempt and ordinary like those we see
in our own homes and in the streets. Others we would try to avoid
in the dark. They are eager to speak: not in their own homes and
not in youth clubs, not even in school, but in a place where straight
talking is hardly encouraged – in the city square, facing the TV
cameras. The young people are bursting to talk, they try to explain
why their lives are so drab and pointless and why they fight each
other all the time. They are obviously dissatisfied with their lives
and are pleased that someone else is concerned and willing to help
them tackle their problems.[1]

These are the opening words of a review article of a live TV
programme from Balashikha, an industrial town some twenty kilo-
metres from Moscow, where gang fights are common and last year a
gang of boys badly beat up some girls.

Since March 1985, when Mikhail Gorbachov took over the Party
leadership, the entire Soviet media have featured revealing information about various aspects of Soviet youth which was previously
known to most readers and researchers, but could not be discussed
openly owing to political constraints. Soviet youth and youth culture
have now been widely publicised. It is the policy of restructuring
(*perestroika*) and openness (*glasnost*) that has made these discussions
possible.

One of the most urgent and vital ideological objectives of this
policy is to achieve speedy change in the political and social outlook
of the Soviet people, which was corroded during Leonid Brezhnev's
administration (1964–82). Gorbachov evidently sees the change in
this 'human factor' as the prime precondition of the country's
economic and social revival. If this transformation is vital for the
public generally, it is all the more important for the younger
generation. The Party has stressed this plainly:

> We must pay more attention to cultivating the work, political-
> ideological and moral education of our young people; and we must
> act swiftly and with more urgent resolve in eliminating everything
> extraneous in our work with youth, especially in the erstwhile

1

didactic tone and administrative methods. Yes, all this does exist
and ought to be mentioned ... there is no other realistic way of
forming an individual, of moulding a young person's civic-
mindedness than his or her own involvement in all public affairs.
There can be no substitute for political experience.[2]

Over the past thirty years, important changes have been taking
place in Soviet youth culture. Many new developments and trends
have emerged. There is clearly considerable concern about the
younger generation and its changing attitudes, particularly the deviant behaviour of many youngsters, the widespread drug abuse and
the increasing juvenile delinquency. In order to understand the
problems and to deal with them effectively, new ideas and methods
have to be developed and based upon full information and free
discussion. The lack of serious research and statistical data in recent
years has resulted in great gaps in sociological studies, including in
youth affairs. As the eminent sociologist Tatiana Zaslavskaya has
written, 'One has to admit that the level of much sociological
research is still very low [and] little effort has been made to promote
fundamental sociological theory.'[3]

Future work on many aspects of Soviet life, including youth
culture, is bound to be hampered by this legacy for some time to
come. This chapter is a modest attempt to review diverse trends in
youth culture based mainly on recent books, articles, press reports
and personal interviews in the USSR.

BACKGROUND TO YOUTH CULTURE

Youth culture has changed dramatically over recent years. The
various political and social changes, and the contradictions that have
accompanied them, have all been reflected in the behaviour of the
younger generation. As two sociologists point out,

> All genuine social processes are being reflected in the problems of
> the younger generation, as if in a mirror. This shows how import-
> ant is its role in society. A vital methodological problem, therefore,
> is analysis of the changes in the social development of the younger
> generation and its relationship to the real contradictions which
> young people face when entering independent life.[4]

The first overt manifestation of independent youth culture
appeared while Khrushchov was pursuing his policy of 'destalin-

isation'. It was a tense period, full of ups and downs, as tentative democratisation produced anxiety and frustration, especialy among young people. Relaxation of political control created conditions conducive to various cultural developments, but these were often frustrated by the rigid framework of official cultural institutions which were inadequate as forums of broad cultural expression. Most young people were eager to move further along the road of political liberalisation and became impatient and defiant when confronted by the old Stalinist bureaucracy. By and large, young people were idealistic; they tended to expect more from the leadership because, at that time, they still firmly believed in socialism.

New cultural developments had a great impact in the country; there was an unprecedented boom in poetry as the younger generation expressed its aspirations for a better future. In poets and bards, new forms of social and political consciousness found expression. Poets like Yevtushenko, Voznesensky, Akhmadulina and Bulat Okudzhava could fill indoor sports stadiums and their young audience was as exhilarated by the poetry as rock music fans in the West were by rock groups. It was a poetry of new dimensions: painfully sincere and desperately optimistic.

Young urban intellectuals provided the vanguard of this movement but, with the appearance of tape-recorders and more poetry publications, the entire country soon became involved. In those days young poets gave readings all over the Soviet Union and their popularity, especially among young people, was enormous.

The newly emergent genre of guitar ballads became popular and the famous poet, bard and satirist Bulat Okudzhava inspired a new movement. His songs were recorded and distributed unofficially, and many young people formed their own guitar-song groups. They met anywhere they could – in parks, gardens, apartments or on street corners; and they were officially frowned upon, although the authorities could do nothing to stop their activities altogether. Moreover, as a Soviet source attests,

> In the late 1950s and early 1960s, young people became totally fascinated by transistor radios. Various pocket circuit diagrams changed hands ... Youngsters who were more daring and inventive began to make their own transistors and recordings.[5]

Thus commenced the 'first wave' of unofficial popular youth culture.

Although the authorities arranged public discussions for young people, many youngsters began to form their own small discussion groups where the range of topics was unrestricted. Even military cadets and young officers took part in this movement. Needless to say, the authorities forced many groups to disband.

Students formed independent satirical theatres out of which grew popular clubs for quiz games and other self-entertainment. There were also independent clubs for outdoor recreation, domestic travel, body building and combat sports, popular music, and so on. In general, the independent culture of Soviet youth at the time developed on the basis of indigenous cultural roots; the influence of Western youth culture was still relatively small, largely because of the complete cultural and ideological isolation of the country during Stalin's and Khrushchov's administration.

Most manifestations of unofficial youth culture were quite constructive, idealistic and humanist. Political development after the fall of Khrushchov, therefore, must be seen in terms of the destruction and disillusionment of youthful idealism. In so far as previous political and social experience had shown young people the possibility of attaining genuine political and social awareness, many young people joined dissident groups at the end of the 1960s, when the political situation under Brezhnev deteriorated.

All the same, unless they had been inherent in the system in the first place, the Brezhnev ideological regime could not have engendered so many adverse developments and exposed such fundamental contradictions in such a relatively short time. Yet over the last two decades, the younger generation seems to have felt, more than ever before, the 'hypocrisy, artificiality and dishonesty' of the lifestyles of the older generation – those seemingly intelligent, refined and good-natured people, the former 'romantic' youth of the 1960s.[6] Young people became acutely aware of two sides of life: the 'facade' and the 'inside'; and they became alienated from society, experiencing 'loneliness', social as well as psychological.[7]

During those years, most of the institutions for official youth culture (primarily the Komsomol) became exceedingly formal and bureaucratic, endeavouring merely to implement the dominant Party ideology (see Chapter 2). Needless to say, the younger generation turned away from them and the gap between official and unofficial youth culture grew wider all the time.

Thanks to the relaxation of relations with the West during the period of *détente*, this ever-growing vacuum was gradually filled by Western youth culture, with its rock music, trends and fashions, and its consumerist, hedonistic ideology. Various Western youth subcultures, like mods and rockers, skinheads and bikers, found their eager imitators among Soviet youth, with all the sartorial garb, artefacts, 'bricolage' and, sometimes, even their macho, racist and semi-fascist ideology. Consequently, many young people developed a defiant attitude towards official Soviet ideology and expressed it quite openly. A *Komsomolskaya pravda* correspondent recently quoted a letter from a youth group in Rostov: 'We are not afraid to admit that we are the most overt contras. In other words, we are your mortal enemies.'[8]

This hiatus between official and unofficial ideology was aggravated by the increasingly complex socio-economic conditions which the younger generation was having to cope with in the 1970s. The demographic situation was changing consideraby under the impact of rapid scientific and technical progress. The large migration of rural dwellers into towns (at the rate of some 1.5 million a year) was putting a severe strain upon the urban infrastructure, which could not cope. The distribution of the young population also developed unevenly, with the result that the lowest percentage of young people eligible for work is currently located in the old industrial belt of the Russian Federation, the three Baltic Republics and the Ukraine. These areas had experienced the greatest fall in birth rate after the Second World War, especially during the last thirty years. These are the industrial regions, however, which contain the largest percentage of traditional labour-intensive industries. Academician Aganbegyan has pointed out that in the USSR, 'about fifty million people are involved in manual labour: approximately every third person in industry, every second in construction, and three out of four workers in agriculture'.[9]

So the psychological and social pressures on the younger generation, which has been encouraged to complete higher education and gain good jobs on the one hand, yet has been offered only manual work on the other, has undoubtedly been very great.

The so-called 'demographic war echo' or 'demographic waves' or 'demographic holes' are also likely to complicate economic development for a long time and, no doubt, will produce various administrative restrictions upon population migration, access to higher and vocational education, and housing policy. Moreover, the younger generation is steadily being outnumbered by the older one, especially in the above-mentioned areas. Thus, as Shubkin points out: 'All this means that in the very near future the younger generation will have to shoulder the burden of additional work responsibilities far more than the previous generation did; yet it is not equipped morally or psychologically for the task.'[10]

Insufficient socio-political integration of young people, which Gorbachov has mentioned, is also leading to generation conflict manifesting itself in a number of ways. As Karl Mannheim once said of such conflict,

> Within a youthful generation there are groups which work up the material of their common experience in different ways. The collective experience of specific historical moments is more intense during periods of rapid change. The more rapid the change, the greater the gap between generational sets of consciousness ... Youthful response contains positive and creative qualities.[11]

This appears to be the case in the Soviet Union today and is certainly causing serious conflict.

YOUTH CULTURE TODAY

In the USSR the 1970s and 1980s have witnessed the emergence of various unofficial youth groups. In contrast to youth groups in earlier historical periods, 'never before did belonging to one's group or team mean such a strong subordination of a young person to the group's rules or norms: from tastes in music and fashion to distinctive ways of thinking and expressing oneself, quite incomprehensible to the older generation'.[12] Today one can clearly distinguish two main types of youth associations: the first consists of groups formed on the basis of common interests peculiar to each group and not necessarily on the basis of common territory; the second is formed on a common territorial basis, and the interests of the groups are very often identical. The first type consists of various manifestations of counter-culture, the second of different territorial subcultures. In their own ways, these associations 'call into question the adequacy of dominant cultural ideology'.[13]

The recent Soviet interest in youth groups has brought to light fascinating information and methodological approaches. Youth groups of the counter-culture type are gradually becoming recognised officially and classified under the headings of 'amateur youth associations' (*samodeyatelnye obyedinyeniya molodyozhi – SOM*) and 'informal youth associations' (*neformalnye obyedinyeniya molodyozhi –*

NOM). The complex nature of the groups (especially those of the *NOM* type) and, in some cases, the loose dividing line between them, produce frequent inconsistencies in official attitudes towards them. All the same, it has been stated quite unequivocally that,

> information reaching the editorial office, not only from Moscow, Leningrad or Minsk, but from less obvious towns like Rzhev and Berdsk, shows that the existence of youth groups, particularly teenage gangs, has become a fact of life. They may take different forms; some arouse understandable protest, others merit our sympathy and support. Some have become popular nationwide (like the soccer or rock fans), others remain known only in their own town or even in one district of a town. The groups follow trends in East or West, or they may have indigenous roots. Some emerge for no more than a week or so, others linger for years. One thing is clear: we can no longer ignore this sphere of youth activity.[14]

Many groups have formed around the common interest of members in different forms of rock music: punks, rockers, the System, Zen, heavy metal, break dancing, and so on. And they have generally adopted appropriate fashion, 'argo' and behaviour common to their Western idols. Many of them insist, none the less, that they are non-aggressive, apolitical and democratic and that they are successfully assimilating Western rock music into Soviet conditions.

Soccer fans call themselves '*fanaty*' and follow their soccer team round the country; each group has a leader respected for knowledge of the game and qualities as an organiser with 'charisma'. The 'fans' often claim they are not aggressive, do not approve of drinking and hooliganism, yet they are known to have been involved in fights and vandalism, as the part-documentary film *It Isn't Easy to be Young* revealed. The fans seem to have worked out their own membership rules, and one of the most popular graffiti is: 'I want to be a fan'. Girls as well as boys are among the soccer fans.

Punks are reported to be on the decline and many have joined the 'System'. Some 'System' members have also begun to take an interest in social problems, calling themselves 'Optimists'. Such afficionados frequently disagree with one another, sometimes on 'macho' issues, such as whether girls should be allowed to join.[15]

The youth group known as the 'Firm' consists of theatre buffs and is divided into two sections: one consisting of young people for whom theatre going is a hobby, the other made up of amateur experts of theatrical performance. Such people are also often members of unofficial amateur theatre studios which in Moscow alone number over two hundred. Both groups compete for tickets and have developed a code of conduct – 'squeezing' each other out of queues without using violence: 'we ban fights and use pressure instead.'[16]

There are also youth groups that form around common 'literary' interests. One is called the 'Devotees of Bulgakov', its members meeting in an apartment of the building described in Mikhail Bulgakov's novel *Master and Margarita*. The scene is described as follows:

> A company of between 30 and 40 teenagers behaved quite peacefully, with some singing and playing guitars, some philo-sophising, some playing the parts of Azazello, Korovyov and other characters in the book. Yet there was something else about them that struck the observer: 'satanism' was a constant theme of most of their songs, jokes and conversation. It was actually an artificial mixture of mysticism and biting satire on present-day life.[17]

Most members of these groups appear to be young men and women who want to develop their intellectual, cultural, sporting, social and other interests. They may or may not come from the same area of town or the same social group. Although young people from a white-collar background seem to constitute a majority, they all conduct free discussions and usually meet regularly, not only because they need social contact, but also because they need to share or exchange their tapes, artefacts and other bricolage peculiar to each group – material that is not sold in shops.

The great scarcity of commodities for this youthful activity creates an additional reason for the existence of such groups. In general, the groups are not aggressive and, as a member of the 'System' puts it, 'Aggression is not in fashion any more.'[18] Their erstwhile semi-clandestine existence compelled members to adopt nom de plumes connected with their hobby or interest – for example, Azazello, Pierro, Primus. To each other, however, they are often known as 'Homo-Nomo' (a play on the Russian acronym for 'informal youth association' and analogous to homo sapiens).[19] Many groups and their members, despite growing official sympathy and understanding towards them, are still at best ignored, at worst victimised. For that reason, 'an individual tries to find various ways of releasing energy because the straight road is either closed or filled with many warning signs. In the end, we give up and have to try a circuitous route.'[20]

Formation of informal youth groups (the *NOM*) depends on a common territory (street, housing estate, city suburb) or on a number of young people of the same age group. The groups are reasonably permanent, largely male and have a very strict hierarchical structure. They commonly assemble in the evenings to patrol their territory and sometimes terrorise young people who do not belong in their ranks. Many are involved in using and supplying drugs, toxic materials and black market goods. Although most members are teenagers at school or technical college, their leaders (known as 'kings') are often older and more experienced (some have criminal records). Frequently, competing local groups fight for control of the common territory and are involved in vandalism and petty crime. A journalist has described their lives as follows,

> This life, sometimes bitter and stupid, is the only one they know. All else is sheer boredom! This situation started at a time when our schools, Pioneer clubs, sports clubs and all formal organisations, in sociological terms, became totally bureaucratic and inhibitive, mainly because everything in them was banned – even to be a child with an unpredictable nature. What did it lead to? Children deserted these child-centred institutions and formed their own territory wherever possible – on the streets, in the tenements, sometimes in private homes, everywhere, but always in the shadows, in the direct and indirect sense of the word.[21]

Some young people come together for an evening or weekend simply out of a desire to pass the time. Out of boredom they then commit petty crimes or, under the influence of alcohol, they become involved in fights. Drugs seem to be used often, and it is known that particularly cruel criminal acts are committed as a result of psycho-pathological behaviour.[22]

It is difficult exactly to determine the social composition of *NOM* groups from existing information. Much research still has to be done. But it is evident from reports that they seem to form mainly in the industrial suburbs of large towns, in new housing developments and in medium or small smokestack cities. These are the areas where official institutions for young people are either insufficient and function badly, or do not function at all. It has been suggested that acute social and economic disparity – between large cities, on the one hand, and medium and small towns, on the other, and between urban and rural life – has given rise to a feeling of discontent among the population of underprivileged areas. The youth of industrial suburbs and small towns is expressing this discontent by direct confrontation with young people of large cities, especially with those who are more conspicuous in their exclusive forms of cultural consumption. The 'conservative Sovietism' of these young people is said to be the ideological subterfuge which they use as intimidation together with violence (see Chapter 6).[23]

According to media reports, the range of subcultural activity is extensive:

> The scope of senseless activity is enormous; it accommodates a variety of tastes: skirmishing and even full-blown battles, all manner of dubious adventures, a variety of drug-taking, gambling with huge stakes and hostility between rival youth gangs ... This is an entire generation of young people from the age of ten to almost thirty, and it constitutes tens of millions of people.[24]

Commentators point out that social and economic losses sustained by society through this 'youthful excess' are extremely high, and various ways of tackling the problem have been suggested, including lowering the legal age of employment and temporary employment. The average age of commencing work is as high as 20–21, and many young people seem to view work as a necessary evil, 'an inevitable tragedy'. In a recent survey of senior form pupils, it was discovered that only 5 per cent intended to go straight into work on leaving school.[25]

EDUCATION AND *PERESTROIKA*

The unprecedented development of subcultural activity has not only resulted from the failure of official culture and the Komsomol. The schools and the education system as a whole in the last twenty years have not provided the younger generation with proper moral and spiritual education because of their authoritarian and bureaucratic structure, and the hostility and high-handedness of teachers. Moreover, the growing emphasis on science and technology in the school curriculum has undermined the teaching of the humanities. As a result, pupils have become alienated and disillusioned, especially those less successful academically. As the writer Chingiz Aitmatov has complained in *Pravda*,

> The technocratic approach and decline in the humanitarian way of thinking have become painfully apparent. But humanism depends

on how far we value the human notion of social responsibility, social equality, truth, sincerity and kindness in everything we do.[26]

An overemphasised orientation on academic education at the expense of practical industrial training has further exaggerated the already strong prejudice against non-academic jobs. What is more, the introduction of compulsory secondary education up to the age of 17 and the encouragement of young people to take further education have raised the average age of young people entering working life (see above). In the circumstances of extensive economic development which required a great deal of manual labour, feelings of frustration and dissatisfaction developed among youngsters who could not gain more prestigious work or even employment to match their high-level training. What is probably more important, and this has been pointed out many times in the media, is that the process of selection of the 'best' children for schools for music, ballet, mathematics, art and sport – the 'children with prospects' or the 'future stars' – has been an important function of educational institutions. As a result, large numbers of 'ordinary' children were left to feel themselves second rate with only 'the street as their proving ground'.[27]

The rise in the divorce rate (to one in every two marriages in the major cities) and the gradual disintegration of the former extended family relationships have created an atmosphere of family alienation among many young people. Along with many other social factors, this has created a basis for youth subcultural activity. As Brake observes,

> Subcultures arise as attempts to resolve collectively experienced problems resulting from contradictions of social structure and they generate a form of collective identity from which an individual identity can be achieved outside that ascribed by class, education and occupation.[28]

This appears to be what has been happening in the Soviet Union in recent years.

The policy of *perestroika* is intended to engender a moral and ideological transformation in people's consciousness; the issue of youth stands at the very centre of the policy. It is by no means going to be easy to implement. After all, '*Perestroika* not only takes place in the entire system of social relations, it also produces fierce struggles between those who are "for" and those who are "against". This fact more than anything demonstrates the revolutionary nature of current events.'[29]

The present gradual removal of former 'distortions' in ideology and the introduction of more democratic norms into social and political life are obviously affecting youth culture. The first shift in this direction is an overall change in official attitudes towards youth subcultures and youth behaviour in favour of a more understanding and sympathetic approach. The best example of this is the Latvian film *It Isn't Easy to be Young*, which revealed the complex circumstances of contemporary Soviet life in which the younger generation has to find its place and future. The film contains scenes showing the acute moral and psychological problems experienced by young people, including young soldiers returning from Afghanistan. One reviewer wrote that he thought 'this film is superb because everything in it is so truthful'.[30]

Recognition of the creative potential in youth is none the less limited when it comes to 'high' culture, inasmuch as the established cultural elite is vigorously defending its privileged position. The January 1987 Young Artist Exhibition in Moscow clearly illustrated the problem. The exhibition, which was open to artists representing various art styles, was popular with the public and warmly welcomed by 'official representatives of the administrative agencies in charge of culture'. All the same, as one critic records, some artists were irritated 'by all the novelties created by *perestroika* and introduced into the stagnant atmosphere of artistic life, and they did not accept the Exhibition. Representatives of the USSR Academy of Arts, for example, did not even bother to take part in the discussions and ignored their invitations.'[31]

Similarly, in 1986 the Moscow Rock Laboratory wrote to the Union of Soviet Composers asking for professional advice and help. Needless to say, the letter was still awaiting reply in mid-1988.[32] These cultural elites in many cases had produced a great deal of second-rate cultural products and had lost influence with the younger generation over the years.

The changing attitudes towards young people and the transformation of official youth culture are evident in the setting up of new youth clubs and the opening of non-alcoholic cafes, discos, theatre studios, video-cafes and rock music laboratories, as well as the organisation of public rock and jazz concerts and festivals, exhibitions of popular art and various poetry readings (still popular, but not as much as in the 1960s – see Chapter 3). The slow pace of these innovations, however, is resulting in a situation in which many young people still have nothing to do and nowhere to go of an evening or weekend. As a Komsomol commentator reports,

It seems we cannot expect any fall in popularity of unofficial youth associations in the near future. Many of the young people we interviewed expressed dissatisfaction with the official organisation of youth leisure and as many as 60 per cent of *NOM* members stated they would remain members even if state amateur youth clubs were to be set up for them.[33]

Reasons for youth subcultural activities are of a complex social and political nature and clearly require further investigation.

A second technological wave in youth culture has already produced new forms of association:

There are home-made video recordings of rock music. Young people are gathering at home with video equipment, watching and exchanging video cassettes, debating the advantages of video-rock music, though rarely reaching common agreement. So they come together again and again. Evidently the amateur clubs are moving in a new direction[34]

The Soviet Union's technological lag behind the West and the relatively low level of video equipment production open doors to a black market in Western video cassettes with all their ideological and moral influences, just as happened with rock music in the 1970s. Western video cluture is entering the Soviet Union through the 'back door'. It is freely admitted that 'These technological achievements are international in character; those who are ahead have greater opportunities to influence young people in the sphere of leisure, free time and education.'[35] The problem for the Soviet Union is that for some time to come video equipment is likely to remain the exclusive possession of relatively few people, usually the privileged stratum in big cities, and the development of video culture will only aggravate the already uneven distribution of cultural and education benefits.[36]

There are clear signs now, however, of the development of a third technological wave in youth culture – home-made computers. This has given rise to amateur computer clubs which in turn develop into unofficial commercial computer associations that provide services to a range of private customers. The importance of independent computer associations 'lies in their flexibility, professionalism and the efficient functioning of their links ... but it is also apparent that computer programmes can be an ideological weapon.'[37] It is this latter worry that causes the authorities to be ambivalent about expanding its computer industry. Just as the development of photocopying equipment involves the prospect of people duplicating whatever literature they wish, so promoting computer technology has major strategic and political implications.

The policy of *perestroika* aims at raising the country's technological level, speeding up economic growth and enhancing people's ideological commitment. It faces substantial difficulties. The country's economic performance has to improve considerably as quickly as possible for the policy to start to be successful; yet the economy is still operating mainly by the old methods. As a Soviet economist has pointed out, 'We have to introduce change into the mechanism of economic performance without halting the economy's march ahead. We cannot, figuratively speaking, move out of our home to speed up its repair.'[38]

The issue of disaffection of the younger generation has to be resolved soon because acceleration of the economy depends, at least in the immediate future, on young people. The inadequate technological level of industry and agriculture requires a large labour force, and young people are the only source of new labour (the village and domestic sector has been almost totally exhausted). The younger generation has to be willing to endure these pressures for years to come; that is why the question of youth culture and ideology are occupying such an important place in the process of *perestroika*.

Notes

1. Akonova, L., 'Ts. T. stavit problemu', *Trud*, 13 January 1987, p. 3.
2. Gorbachov, M. S., 'The way ahead: more democracy and openness', quoted in the *Guardian*, 22 February 1987, p. 24.
3. Zaslavskaya, T., 'Perestroika v sotsiologii', *Pravda*, 6 February 1987, p. 2.
4. Cherednichenko, G. and Shubkin, V., *Molodyozh vstupaet v zhizn* (Moscow: Mysl, 1985) p. 4.
5. Makarevich, E., 'V ozhidanii tretei volny', *Molodoi kommunist*, 1987, no. 1, p. 20.
6. Marinicheva, O., 'Metalichesky malchik', *Komsomolskaya pravda*, 29 January 1987, p. 4.
7. Ibid.
8. Radov, A., 'Deti detochkina', *Komsomolskaya pravda*, 17 October 1986, p. 2.
9. Aganbegyan, A., 'Na putyakh obnovleniya', *Literaturnaya gazeta*, 18 February 1987, p. 13.

10. Cherednichenko and Shubkin, *Molodyozh vstupaet v zhizn* (note 4), p. 14.
11. Quoted in Brake, M., *Comparative Youth Culture* (London: Routledge & Kegan Paul, 1985) p. 25.
12. Shchekochikhin, Yu., 'Po nam zvonit kolokolchik', *Sotsiologicheskie issledovaniya*, 1987, no. 1, p. 89.
13. Brake, *Comparative Youth Culture* (note 11), p. 21.
14. Shchekochikhin, Yu., 'Na perekryostke', *Literaturnaya gazeta*, 22 October 1986, p. 13.
15. Ibid.
16. Ibid.
17. Kulikov, V., 'Gomo NOMO zhdyot vnimaniya', *Molodoi kommunist*, 1986, no. 12, p. 25.
18. Shchekochikhin, 'Na perekryostke'.
19. Kulikov, 'Gomo NOMO zhdyot vnimaniya', (note 17), p. 25.
20. Shchekochikhin, 'Na perekryostke'.
21. Radov, 'Deti detochkina' (note 8).
22. Borin, A., 'Skuka', *Literaturnaya gazeta*, 24 October 1986, p. 12.
23. Shchekochikhin, Yu., 'Allo, my vas slyshim', *Literaturnaya gazeta*, 8 April 1987, p. 13.
24. Radov, A., 'Bezdelniki ponevole', *Komsomolskaya pravda*, 11 March 1987, p. 2.
25. Chernyak, I., 'Uroki "bezmozolnoi" pedagogiki', *Sobesednik*, November 1987, no. 48, pp. 4–5.
26. Aitmatov, C., 'Veryu v cheloveka', *Pravda*, 14 February 1987, p. 3.
27. Plutnik, A., 'Na okraine', *Izvestiya*, 22 March 1987, p. 3.
28. Brake, *Comparative Youth Culture* (note 11), p. ix.
29. Zaslavskaya, 'Perestroika v sotsiologii' (note 3).
30. Kuchkina, O., 'Chestnoi kameroi', *Komsomolskaya pravda*, 8 January 1987, p. 2.
31. Vishnyakov, V., 'Zritel golosuet "za"', *Trud*, 14 January 1987, p. 4.
32. 'Kommentariy gruppy Vadima Vavilova', *Sobesednik*, January 1987, no. 2, p. 14.
33. Kulikov, 'Como Nomo ...' (note 17), p. 26.
34. Makarevich, 'V ozhidanii ...' (note 5), p. 22.
35. Ibid., pp. 25–6.
36. Vilchek, V., 'Poka dzhin ne vypushchen iz kassety', *Yunost*, 1987, no. 3, pp. 78–80.
37. Makarevich, 'V ozhidanii ...' (note 5), p. 26.
38. Popov, G. 'Perestroika v ekonomike', *Pravda*, 20 January 1987, p. 2.

2 The Komsomol
Jim Riordan

The older generation often does not know how to deal properly with young people who are bound to approach socialism *differently*, by a *different* route, a *different* form, in *different* circumstances. That is why, incidentally, we have to be unreservedly in favour of the youth league's *organisational independence*, and *not just* because the opportunists are scared of that independence. Without complete independence young people *will not be able* either to make good socialists or to prepare themselves for taking socialism forward.

V.I. Lenin[1]

Not to put too fine a point on it: the Communist Youth League (*Kommunistichesky soyuz molodyozhi* – Komsomol) is in crisis. Widely accused of being staffed by careerists and time-servers, of forcing young people to join by threats to their careers, of tedium and formalism in its political training, of, as Mikhail Gorbachov has put it, 'marching down one side of the street while young people are walking down the other in the opposite direction', it has clearly lost control over many, if not the bulk of, Soviet young people, as well as their confidence and respect.

Its future is in dispute. The open and revealing debate on it now in progress in the media is providing new perspectives on the Komsomol, as well as on the youth ferment that has precipitated many of the changes underway in Soviet society.

BRIEF HISTORY

The Bolsheviks had no youth organisation before the October 1917 Revolution. Nor had any other Russian political party. But the Bolsheviks were well aware of the potency of youth in and after revolution. As Lenin put it, 'young people ... will decide the outcome of the entire struggle'.[2] And on the eve (August) of the Revolution, Bukharin reported to the Sixth Party Congress on 'youth organisations': 'when the direct struggle for socialism begins, the

Party will pay the utmost attention to establishing revolutionary Bolshevik youth organisations'. Significantly, the resolution adopted called for 'independent organisations, not subordinate organisationally, only spiritually linked with the Party'.[3]

Although youth 'factions' had been attached to the first workers' councils (Soviets) in 1905 at Orekhovo-Zuevo, the birth of the Komsomol is officially set as the autumn of 1918. Between 29 October and 4 November 1918, 194 delegates representing as many as 120 different youth groups met in Moscow at the first Komsomol Congress. While the Congress expressed 'solidarity with the Russian Communist Party [Bolsheviks]', it also declared the Komsomol 'an independent organisation'.[4] Indeed, its first rules reiterated that it was a 'fully independent organisation' whose activities were based on 'the principle of complete freedom of action'.[5] Such autonomy was not to last long under Civil War conditions. In the following year, the word 'independent' was erased and, at the Third Congress, held in October 1920 and at which Lenin spoke, the 'freedom of action' principle disappeared.

Similarly, initial relative freedom of election to top posts gave way to Party control of nomination. Up to 1920, members elected the Central Committee by voting for nominees individually; and since there were more nominees than posts, an element of choice obtained. In 1920 the choice was removed: delegates to the Third Congress were presented with a single list of nominees drawn up in advance by the Party, with only one nominee for each vacancy. Delegates had to vote on the list *as a whole*.

From then on until today, no real elections have taken place, not only to the Central Committee but, as we shall see below, to secretaryships of local committees as well. In fact, from its Central Committee down to its smallest branch, the Komsomol has functioned under direct Party tutelage; and since the leading Komsomol officials are themselves Party members, they have always been subject to Party discipline and removable on Party command. One Komsomol leader, Alexander Kosarev, was even a member of the Party Politburo. All first secretaries (the *de facto* leaders) of the Komsomol have been automatically coopted on to the Party Central committee, and all ideology secretaries to candidate membership of the Party Central Committee.

If that were not enough to ensure Party control, the Party has over the years arbitrarily removed Komsomol officials and leadership whenever it has wished; that includes the mass arrest and execution of virtually the entire Komsomol leadership during the Stalin purge years (of the first seven Komsomol leaders between 1918 and 1938, six were shot and one, Milchakov, spent 18 years (1938–1956) in a Magadan labour camp – (see Table 2.1).

Table 2.1 First Secretaries of the Komsomol (1918–88)

Yefim Tsetlin (Nov.–Dec. 1918) – shot
Oscar Ryvkin (1919–21) – shot
Lazar Shatskin (1921–22) – shot
Pyotr Smorodin (1922–24) – shot
Nikolai Chaplin (1924–28) – shot
Alexander Milchakov (1928–29) – arrested, but survived
Alexander Kosarev (1929–38) – shot
Nikolai Mikhailov (1938–52)
Alexander Shelepin (1952–58)
Vladimir Semichastny (1958–59)
Sergei Pavlov (1959–68)
E. M. Tyazhelnikov (1968–77)
Boris Pastukhov (1977–82)
Victor Mishin (1982–86)
Victor Mironenko (1986–)

Sources:　*Bolshaya sovetskaya entsiklopediya*; Medvedev, Roy, *Let History Judge* (London: Macmillan, 1972) pp. 208–9; Kosarev, Alexander, *Sbornik vospominaniy* (Moscow: Molodaya gvardia, 1963); *Vozhaki Komsomola. Sbornik* (Moscow: Molodaya gvardia, 1978); *Sobesednik*, July 1986, no. 30, p. 2; *Molodoi Kommunist*, 1988, no. 9, p. 38.

NB:　　　The fate of the first seven Komsomol leaders was admitted publically only 50 years after their 'repression'. See Klyukin, V., 'Sekretar Tsk', *Komsomolskaya pravda*, 11 June 1988, pp. 2–3.

Although the principle of Komsomol organisation, 'democratic centralism', was from the outset far more centralist than democratic, and has remained so right up to the present, early Komsomol meetings gave vent to dissention and the initial congresses produced many divided votes. Even during the early 1920s, the Komsomol in its activities was still relatively independent, as Ralph Fisher attests in his history of Komsomol congresses: 'Komsomolites were still able to disagree openly on moderately consequential issues; they could still register dissenting votes; and their sharp criticism of arbitrary rule within the League could still be spread in the published record.'[6]

Even this limited freedom to demur vanished by the mid-1920s. The Komsomol could not dare question in the slightest degree the supreme authority of the Party; voting on all issues became mechanical and any dissenters (or even supposed dissenters) were removed. The Komsomol was the first organisation to be purged (for its alleged 'Trotskyist leanings'). Not even abstentions from voting were recorded at congresses after 1926 – until the 20th Congress in 1987.

Initially the Komsomol was very small – the largest membership during the founding period being some 400 000 – that is, under two per cent of those within the eligible age group, and two-thirds the size of the Party.[7] Like the Party, it aimed to recruit only 'outstanding representatives' and had no pretensions at embracing all young people, even if that were possible. Although favoured by the ruling Party, it had to vie for members and attention with surviving pre-revolutionary youth organisations like the Boy Scouts, the YMCA, the Jewish Maccabee and various religious youth groups. It was not until 1922 that such rivals were proscribed, although the Seventh Congress in 1926 still mentioned the existence of 'leagues of Christian youth' and other non-communist youth associations.[8] From 1926, however, the Komsomol had the field to itself.

The tasks of the Komsomol were set by the Party as early as March 1919. It was to be a 'source of trained reserves for the Party' and to help the Party implement its policies. It was 'to organise and train young people in a communist manner, to build a communist society and to defend the Soviet Republic'.[9]

In the years to follow, the Komsomol retained many of the characteristics it had acquired under the civil war conditions – its organisational structure based on democratic centralism, its role of replenishing the Party with young recruits, of political socialisation of young people and helping the Party to carry out its policies, as well as its political control by the Party. On the other hand, from being a tiny 'vanguard' of youth, it became a mass organisation; it shifted its organisational base from home to school and workplace. And since the mid-1920s it has had no formal rivals, nor have dissent, independent initiative or free elections been permitted.

In the current debate on the Komsomol's future, reconsideration of the past is constantly providing food for thought on exactly how it evolved as it has and what are the lessons to learn. And that has implications for a review of Soviet history that go beyond immediate relevance to the Komsomol.

ORGANISATIONAL STRUCTURE

The organisational structure of the Komsomol (see Figure 2.1), just like its rules and regulations, is virtually identical to that of the Party.

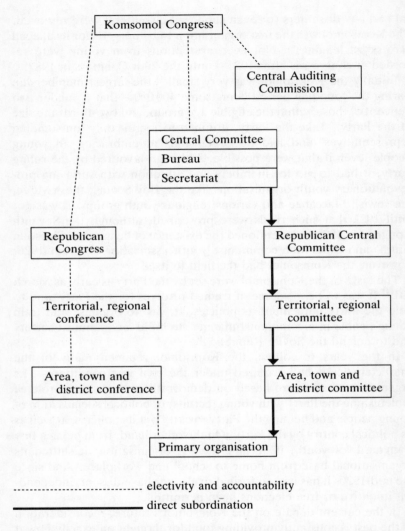

Note: The April 1987 Congress was attended by 500 delegates.
        The Central Auditing Commission had 63 members and an inner
        Bureau of five members.
        The Central Committee had 270 full and 64 candidate members.
        The Bureau had ten members, and the Secretariat ten full and seven
        candidate members.

Figure 2.1   Organisational structure of the Komsomol

Primary Komsomol branches exist at work, school and college where there are at least three members. They hold regular meetings, some of which have been open to all, some closed and restricted to a small band of members.[10] The 20th Komsomol Congress, however, resolved to make all local Komsomol meetings open to everyone – just as local Party meetings were declared to be from mid-1987.

Meetings of the Komsomol elect delegates to the various conferences at which committes (town, district, regional, and so on) are elected. Komsomol congresses are held at Republican and All-Union level, the latter being the highest authority; it meets every five years. In practice, all congress decisions are earlier agreed upon in the Party Central Committee and accepted with applause by Congress delegates. The Congress also chooses a Central Committee and elects a Bureau and a number of secretaries for the Secretariat. The First Secretary, as well as those elected to executive positions at district level and above, are conventionally Party members who continue in the Komsomol even after they have passed the prescribed age limit of 28.[11] In 1982, as many as 72.8 per cent of all officials of regional up to Republican Komsomol bodies were Party members, as were 56.7 per cent of town and district agencies.[12]

Like the Party, the Komsomol is run by paid officials, with no important decisions left to the initiative of ordinary members. Moscow alone was said (in 1987) to have as many as 2700 paid Komsomol officials – more than any central ministry![13]

All members pay a monthy subscription which is largely nominal and progressive: for example, a student on an average monthly grant of 50 rubles pays ten kopeks; a nurse earning average pay of 95 rubles pays 50 kopeks, while those earning over 151 rubles pay 1.5 per cent of their income.[14]

MEMBERSHIP

As its (1985) rules stated, the Komsomol 'is open to progressive young people between the ages of 14 and 28 dedicated to the Soviet homeland'.[15] Somewhat contradictorily, it also aimed 'to encompass and organise the entire younger generation'. After all, 'constant growth in the Komsomol's ranks is a sign of successful activity, a sign of its fitness and authority among young people, a result of constant, patient and individual educational work with every young person.[16]

Despite this 'universal' membership, the Komsomol does have an

initiation procedure which involves applicants in filling in a question-
naire about themselves, answering questions on Party and Komsomol
history, and being proposed by at lest two Komsomol members with a
year-long membership, or by a Party member. True to the old
Bolshevik tradition of Party membership, the Komsomol is therefore
open to 'anyone who accepts Komsomol rules, actively takes part in
building communism, works in a Komsomol organisation, carries out
Komsomol decisions and pays dues'.[17]

Total membership is said to have risen from some 20 000 in 1918 to
40 million in 1987 (see Table 2.2).[18] Only in the last 25 years, however,
has it represented a majority of young people; it is still in the minority
in rural areas. From representing under 2 per cent of the eligible age
group in 1920, it grew to embrace 5 per cent in 1926, 10 per cent in the
mid-1920s, 15 per cent in 1936 and 20 per cent in 1950; the real take-off,
or transition from 'progresive youth' to 'mass membership', occurred
between 1950 and 1956 when membership more than doubled – to 42 per
cent in 1956. The quadrupling of membership between 1950 and 1987
brought it up to 65 per cent of the eligible age group.[19]

Table 2.2   Komsomol membership (1918–88)

Years	Membership
1918	22 100
1920	482 000
1925	1 140 706
1930	2 528 351
1935	3 531 893
1940	10 255 261
1945	7 069 210
1950	10 512 385
1955	18 617 532
1960	18 230 458
1965	22 061 668
1970	25 551 680
1975	33 760 617
1980	39 572 110
1985	41 944 490
1987	40 856 636
1988	38 400 000

Source: *Vsesoyuzny Leninsky Kommunistichesky Soyuz Molodyozhi.
Naglyadnoye posobie* (Moscow: Molodaya gvardia, 1985) p. 39;
Molodoi Kommunist, 1987, no. 10, p. 52; *Sport v SSSR*, 1988,
no. 3, p. 10.

Membership diminishes with age and Soviet sources have provided only vague figures. One source gives 90 per cent of school-leavers (17 year olds) as members,[20] another cites 80 per cent of 16–17 year olds,[21] another over 75 per cent of Komsomol-age schoolchildren.[22] Evidently, a significant number of young people see their *rites de passage* extending only as far as the Pioneers (9–14 year olds). In recognition of this reluctance, in 1987 the Komsomol abandoned its aim to encompass (*okhvat*) all young people; the target set was now 60 per cent of all youth, which brought total membership down to just over 38 million in 1988.[23]

Composition of membership has altered considerably over the years. In the mid-1920s, when over 80 per cent of the population was rural, the proportion of rural Komsomol members was just over half (51 per cent in 1926) of the total membership; by the mid-1950s, when the population was still largely rural, the rural Komsomol percentage was relatively small (13.3 per cent at a time when the rural population was 59 per cent).[24] By the early 1980s, however, it had fallen even more drastically to 6.4 per cent (when the rural population was 35 per cent);[25] it had risen slightly to 7.4 per cent in 1987.[26]

In the early years, the bulk of the membership was male, with females only making up 15 per cent in 1924. Since then the proportion of females has risen, eventually to form a majority: 19 per cent in 1926, 34 per cent in 1936, 42 per cent in 1949, 44.3 per cent in 1954, 51 per cent in 1970 and 53 per cent in 1987 (when 27.9 per cent of Party members were female).[27] Although today young women either dominate or comprise a sizeable minority of lower-level Komsomol posts – 54.1 per cent of secretaries of primary groups, 50.2 per cent of town and district branches, 43.6 per cent of Republican, territorial and regional committees – their numbers dwindle the higher they go. Only 27.2 per cent of all first secretaries at regional and Republican level were women in 1982;[28] and none of the 15 Komsomol leaders have been women. In 1984, a resolution was passed to recruit more young women to Komsomol posts[29] and, in early 1987, Gorbachov spoke of the need to 'promote more women to leading positions'.[30] All the same, the Komsomol is still run primarily by men, especially at the highest levels (the Bureau and Secretariat elected in 1987 had 19 men and three women), although the rise in women's membership and occupancy of lower-level posts is certainly marked.

The age of membership has also shifted markedly over the years: in 1925 only 4 per cent of members were over 23 and all five Komsomol leaders had been under 21; by 1928 some 16 per cent of members were over 23 and, in 1936, about 30 per cent were over 23 – roughly the same percentage as in 1954 when the upper age limit was raised from 26 to 28.[31] In 1982, the age breakdown was as follows: 4.2 per cent were 14, 25.2 per cent were 15–17, 40 per cent were 18–22, 19 per cent were 23–25, 10.8 per cent were 26–28, and 0.8 per cent were over 28. Thus, there was still about 30 per cent of membership over 23 in the early 1980s.[32] Complaints are being increasingly voiced today that the Komsomol is 'ageing', that youngsters are not joining as they used to, and that many full-time officials are over 28 and out of touch with young people of Komsomol age. Significantly, the published statistics only feature primary group secretaries by age: 5.7 per cent were over 28 in 1982.[33] it can be worked out, however, that the averge age of Central Committee members in 1987 was as high as 3.5; the Secretary, Mironenko, was 35 – seven years over the membership age limit.

Educational standards have naturally improved over the last 70 years: in 1924, some two-thirds of delegates to the Congress that year had only a four-year education or less, and not even 1 per cent had gone beyond secondary school. By 1950, however, two-thirds of Congress delegates had completed secondary school and 37.7 per cent had gone on to higher education. In that same year only 16 per cent of membership had secondary or higher education,[34] wheres by 1968 the figure was 40.6 per cent, and in 1982 it was 67.7 per cent.[35] Of full-time officials, all Republican through to regional secretaries had a higher education in 1982; 96 per cent of town and district secretaries had a higher education, and 32.1 per cent of primary group secretaries had a degree.[36] So the Komsomol is run today by well-qualified personnel.

In terms of ethnic composition, there is evidently an attempt at roughly equal representation, reflecting the ethnic proportion in the population at large (see Table 2.3). All fifteen Republics are represented in the Komsomol in 1982 to within a percentage point of their population status, with the exception of the Russians, who are 3.8 per cent down, and the Uzbeks, who are 1.9 per cent up. By 1987 the Russians had fallen another 3.1 per cent. It is noteworthy that the traditionally more economically and culturally advanced ethnic groups (Latvians, Estonians, Russians, Ukrainians) are consistently underrepresented in the Komsomol, whereas the Central Asians and Caucasians are overrepresented in proportion to their share of the total population.

This is almost the reverse of ethnic composition in the Party; the Russian percentage in the Komsomol in 1982 was 11.1 less than in the Party and 3.8 less than in the population, while Ukrainian representation in the Komsomol was 0.8 per cent less than in the Party and 0.9 per cent less than in the population.

Table 2.3   Ethnic composition of the Komsomol (1982 and 1987), population (1982) and the Party (1982)

Nationality	% of Komsomol 1982 (1987)	% of Party	% of population
Russians	48.6 (45.5)	59.7	52.4
Ukrainians	15.2 (15.5)	16.0	16.1
Belorussians	4.0 (4.0)	3.8	3.6
Uzbeks	6.6 (7.2)	2.4	4.7
Kazakhs	3.3 (4.1)	2.0	2.5
Georgians	1.8 (1.8)	1.7	1.4
Azerbaidzhanians	2.8 (3.3)	1.7	2.0
Lithuanians	1.0 (1.1)	0.7	1.0
Moldavians	1.2 (1.3)	0.5	1.1
Latvians	0.4 (0.4)	0.4	0.5
Kirgiz	1.0 (1.3)	0.4	0.7
Tadzhiks	1.3 (1.5)	0.4	1.1
Armenians	2.0 (2.0)	1.5	1.6
Turkmenians	1.0 (1.3)	0.4	0.7
Estonians	0.3 (0.3)	0.3	0.4
Others	9.5 (9.4)	8.1	10.2

Sources: *Vsesoyuzny Leninsky Kommunistichesky Soyuz Molodyozhi. Naglyadnoye posobie* (Moscow: Molodaya gvardia, 1985) p. 46. 'KPSS v tsifrakh', *Partiynaya zhizn*, August 1983, no. 15, p. 23; 'Kartoteka propagandista,' *Molodoi kommunist*, no. 6, 1988, p. 32.

ROLE

The new (1986) Party rules, in the section on 'Party and Komsomol', defines the Komsomol as 'the active assistant and reserve of the Party. It is to help the Party educate young people in a communist spirit, involve them in the practical building of the new society, and shape a generation of all-round developed people ready to work and defend the homeland.'[37]

This neatly sums up the three major roles assigned the Komsomol by the Party since 1918. First, it acts as the Party's agent among young people, carrying out Party policies in industry, farming, the military, education, the social sphere and international affairs. Secondly, it serves as a training ground for future Party members and leaders. Thirdly, it trains, socialises, controls and incorporates young people politically into socialist society.

The shifts in emphasis on the three fundamental roles over the years have reflected the principal stages of Soviet development. While the Civil War necessitated an emphasis on the military, the New Economic Policy switched the focus to education and political instruction. Industrialisation in the late 1920s brought economic tasks to the forefront, collectivisation of agriculture, political guidance of younger children through the Pioneers in school as well as a political offensive against 'enemies of the people' and deviationists. The Second World War naturally brought the military function back into prominence, while post-war reconstruction meant economic campaigns, education and political instruction. In 1987, as a recent list of prime tasks makes clear, the emphasis was on 'organisation of socialist competition, political study, military-patriotic education and lectures'.[38]

In carrying out its work, the Komsomol uses methods similar to those employed by the Party: meetings, talks, lectures, Komsomol schools, and the publication of daily and periodical newspapers and journals and other literature, including the daily *Komsomolskaya pravda* with its circulation of over ten million. The Komsomol owns three publishing houses (publishing in Russian, Ukrainian and Uzbek) with an annual output of over 50 million copies of books and brochures, and in excess of 230 newspapers and magazines for young people, with a total print run of over 82 million copies (see Table 2.4).[39]

The most abiding characteristic is Party control of the Komsomol and, through it, of young people. The whole of Komsomol history is marked by the determination of Party leaders to eliminate anything that appeared to present the slightest hindrance to Party control. As is frequently stressed, the Komsomol's 'strength lies in Party leadership, ideological conviction and dedication to the Party cause.'[40] The top Komsomol body, its Central Committee, is directly subordinate to the Party Central Committee and the local Komsomol group is under local Party supervision. The highest office in the Komsomol, the First Secretary of the Central Committee, is trad-

Table 2.4   Komsomol-published periodicals and printing (000s copies) in 1987

Komsomolskaya pravda	16 685	*Rovesnik*	1 428
Pionerskaya pravda	8 700*	*Tekhnika molodyozhi*	1 783
Molodoi kommunist	803	*Vozhaty*	212
Komsomolskaya zhizn	1 845	*Yuny naturalist*	2 870
Smena	1 040	*Yuny tekhnik*	1 984
Selskaya molodyozh	1 311	*Yuny khudozhnik*	183
Molodaya gvardia	609	*Modelist-Konstruktor*	1 681
Avrora	334	*Pioner*	1 690
Literaturnaya uchoba	17	*Kostyor*	1 147
Studenchesky meridian	687	*Murzilka*	4 952
Druzhba	50*	*Vesyolye kartinki*	9 003
Vokrug sveta	2 591	*Sobesednik*	1 250

Source: Mironenko, V., *Komsomol: initsiativa, tvorchestvo, otvetstvennost* (Moscow: Novosti, 1987) p. 28.

*Figures for 1978.

itionally held by a member of the Party Central Committee and is a Party assignment.

No bones are made about Party control. The Party exercises the control it does 'by selecting, distributing and training Komsomol personnel and by directng the activity of young communists chosen for Komsomol office'.[41]

Since the Komsomol has no official rival among youth organisations, and since it controls state facilities for youth activities – the media, club premises, theatres, sports amenities, and so on – it has only been possible for young people to engage in non-approved activities by setting up an unlawful club and meeting clandestinely. This is precisely what has been happening over the last ten years or so. It was in an attempt to control this situation, which was rapidly getting out of hand, and to bring young people back into the fold, that the Komsomol in 1986 set up 'Youth recreation departments' whose job was to supervise all the 'informal youth groupings and associations'. At the same time, it approved a statute on 'Amateur Associations and Hobby Clubs' in May 1986, which made non-Komsomol clubs legal as long as they had official sponsorship and premises.[42] In practice, they can become legal if they register with the Komsomol which then sponsors them and provides premises. The Leningrad Komsomol had 87 such groups registered in September 1987 and reckoned to increase the number to 300 by 1990.[43]

A further effective means of control by the Komsomol over young people is the 'character reference'. To get on, especially to gain entry to many areas of higher education, school-leavers generally require a reference from the Komsomol. So at least lip service has to be paid to political ideology and passive attendance has to be made at a minimum number of political lectures and Komsomol meetings. Perhaps that is why well over a third (38 per cent) of all Komsomol members were students in 1987.

The *glasnost* policy since mid-1985 has revealed widespread disaffection by young people from Komsomol-led activities and, for the first time since the early 1920s, the setting up of alternative youth groups and, as the eminent sociologist I. S. Kon says, a 'number of youth subcultures'.[44] It has also brought stinging criticism of a wide range of Komsomol affairs, often from within the Komsomol itself. As a leading Party official has admitted, 'In the eyes of the public the Komsomol, which primarily has a duty to tackle youth problems, yet which has generally been unable to tackle anything, has steadily lost trust and authority.[45] In order to regain authority with and control over young people, the Komsomol will radically need to overhaul its organisation and activities. Its leader Victor Mironenko admits this: 'We all recognise the need for a radical restructuring of the Komsomol . . . and a democratising of our internal affairs.[46] All the same, in a poll of Komsomol members in ten areas of the country undertaken by the Higher Komsomol School in 1987, it was found that only 5.3 per cent believed that such a restructuring was actually underway in their branches.[47] Evidently, it is not going to be easy to shift the cumbersome Komsomol machine or take away the *frais de représentation* of its officials.

There now follows an examination of criticism of the Komsomol and an assessment of likely developments.

CRITICISM OF THE KOMSOMOL

Leadership

The common charge in respect of the Komsomol hierarchy is that too many cynical careerists and time-servers are using the organisation merely as a stepping stone to higher things – in government and Party. When *Sobesednik*, the weekly supplement to the daily *Komsomolskaya pravda*, invited readers in September 1986 to express their views on 'sensitive issues of Komsomol activity', thousands wrote in, many not mincing their words about what they thought of their leaders.[48] Igor Chernyak, the journal's head of communist youth education, complained of the 'Komsomol leader in his black limousine and three-piece suit who turns up at *subbotniks* [voluntary work days] just to declame about the public-spiritedness of youth . . . It is time to speak the unpalatable truth to Komsomol bureaucrats, lackeys and time-servers, all those for whom the Komsomol is a step on life's self-propelled escalator . . . you can't carry on like that!'[49]

Others complain of the material privileges that 'bosses' in all walks of life, including the Komsomol, give themselves. A letter to *Pravda* in early 1986 condemned so-called communists who flouted Lenin's insistence on modesty: 'In talking of social justice, we cannot close our eyes to the way Party, local government, trade union, economic and *even Komsomol officials* . . . take advantage of all sorts of special canteens, department stores and hospitals' [author's italics].[50]

Letters to the press talk of the 'faceless grey mass that has filled Komsomol city and district committees for years'.[51] In early 1987 Chernyak returned to the attack on Komsomol bureaucrats who threaten Gorbachov's reforms. They are

> the manipulators, essentially aliens among their own people who are doubly dangerous: their weapon is phrase-mongering, hypocrisy and glossing over reality. They speak the right words, yet smooth over the acuteness of real issues, they call upon others to work, yet are idle themselves, they make our appeals sound trite and people mistrustful of change . . . They are ever ready to report that restructuring is over, all that remains is to reap the fruits of victory. But while these windbags hold forth about change, life stands still.[52]

The Komsomol's own theoretical journal *Molodoi kommunist* wrote of Komsomol secretaries acting as mere 'errand boys' for the Party and the Komsomol being a 'firebrigade' used to douse flare-ups caused by artless economic planners.[53] The same issue gave space to a young man, 'Stalker', who claimed that 'If you take the average youngster and ask whose actions he finds more acceptable – those of a Komsomol official reading a speech on the need for peace, or those of unofficial groups who read no speeches, just write the word Peace on a wall – the answer won't favour the former.'[54]

The situation is worsened by obsession with *political ideology* and *control*. For example, in the collection of documents issued by the Komsomol during 1984, as many as forty-six of the fifty-six resolutions were concerned with 'ideological-political and organisational work'.[55] Agendas for Komsomol meetings are handed down from above, as a result of which 'no one takes them as live' and, 'if the secretary did not dash out early to block the exit, over half the members would escape. We hold meetings for the sake of it, for the notorious "tick" on the report. We vote for measures which we know beforehand we won't carry out and have no intention of doing so.'[56]

But it is not only a matter of local branches being stifled by control from above; up until now they have even had secretaries imposed upon them, with no pretence at democracy or heeding of local opinion. No wonder young people have grown contemptuous of the election farce. Secretaries are,

> literally foisted on members with no regard for their views. It is no secret that in most Komsomol branches the leader is selected beforehand to fit the bill ... Hence the boredom at election meetings and conferences, the utter indifference to what is being said. Everyone knows it has all been decided beforehand, behind closed doors. What sort of democracy is that? Leaders should not be appointed from above, we should elect them by open voting with all Komsomol members taking part and, moreover, with several candidates to choose from.[57]

This process has already begun both spontaneously and as an official experiment. *Sovetsky soyuz* reports 'experiments' at two big plants in the West Siberian town of Noyabrsk, where Komsomol members elected a leader from three candidates.[58] As one Komsomol member said, 'it was as if the dam had burst'.[59] Meanwhile, young workers on the BAM (*Baikal-Amur Magistral*) Siberian railway had been having open elections for all Komsomol secretaries since 1984. But some have not awaited official approval for holding elections. A school student in his final year reports that his Komsomol group voted in a whole new bureau, 'not on the formal principle, but on the basis of genuine leadership'.[60] Another student calls for 'quarterly accountability' of all officials and the right of recall of secretaries who do not justify membership expectations'.[61]

There is still a long way to.go. So far the open elections are only being officially permitted on a small experimental basis and much has to be done 'to make meetings open and honest, to have complete truth and sincerity in our relations, in a word, to be able to run things ourselves with no themes banned from discussion'.[62] Little change has occurred in the Komsomol hierarchy. Three members (out of

334) of the Central Committee were removed in November 1985,[63] and after a relatively brief period as leader, the Brezhnev appointee Victor Mishin moved sideways in July 1986 to the trade unions, to make way for the then 33 year old Victor Mironenko, previously head of the Ukrainian Komsomol Central Committee. In the relatively short time he has been in office, Mironenko has campaigned for minor reforms to Komsomol structure, but without yet actually accomplishing any radical overhaul of the organisation, personnel or methods of work.

Political education

A major reason for the widening rift between young people and the Komsomol is what they perceive as the bossy, crude and excessively moralistic tone of political sermonising indulged in by Komsomol officials. This has resulted in many young people being turned off politics, patriotism, atheism and civic-mindedness, paying lip service to the 'catechism' taught them by the Komsomol. As a Soviet source has put it, 'some people regard political ideas as formulae which, as in mathematics, have to be learned off pat for the next test'.[64]

Forcing young people to attend ideological pep-talks is not the best way of winning converts;

> We're forced to attend (a Komsomol meeting) and hear some report read out monotonously from a scrap of paper. If we don't go we get a rap over the knuckles or our history master gives us low marks. The meeting is boring, everyone does what they like, especially in the back rows where the platform can't see you. The Komsomol doesn't give a damn about providing anything of interest; we don't have any interesting socials. In any case, we've nowhere to hold them.[65]

The trouble is often that Komsomol officials have been more attuned to fulfilling the plan or quota than worrying about the response of members to political propaganda (which they often give no thought to themselves). One such quota set each Komsomol committee is for subscription to periodicals. A Komsomol secretary at a garment making factory in the Altai complains of having to dispose of her compulsory quota of fifteen copies of *Komsomolskaya pravda*, five of *Molodyozh Altaya*, two of *Komsomolskaya zhizn* and one *Molodoi kommunist* (though her members prefer *Rabotnitsa, Krestyanka, Trud*, and *Izvestiya*).[66]

It is increasingly recognised that the former didactic tone, the stressing of the ideal rather than the actual, the denial of reality, the blaming of ills on dark, outside forces, the demand for total commitment from all young people to Komsomol values and activities, the contempt for ideological opponents, and so on, have prevented the Komsomol from dealing successfuly with the demands and aspirations of increasingly curious, restless and sophisticated young people born not only in the post-Stalin era, but in the post-Khrushchov era too. Not only has this policy driven young people away from politics, it has forced some to form their own independent Marxist, socialist and Soviet history study groups. As the Deputy Head of the Komsomol has written, they have 'gathered to study the Marxist classics for themselves and work out what Marx, Engels and Lenin were all about, as well as to analyse Soviet history using these notions'.[67] One of the leaders of the extra-Komsomol socialist movement, Boris Kagarlitsky, himself expelled from the Komsomol and imprisoned in the early 1980s for 'Eurocommunist views', has written that,

> Protest against corruption and alienation of the personality calls forth a keen demand for new, democratic forms of collectivism . . . The initiative was not a response to any appeal from above. Independently of the will of the leadership, a new cultural milieu began to be formed already in the first half of the eighties . . . As in the West in the sixties, interest has increased sharply in both Marxism and utopian socialism.[68]

But the overwhelming response to Komsomol hypocrisy and cant is plainly sheer indifference. The former Belorussian Komsomol First Secretary, Vasily Dragovets, writing in *Molodoi kommunist*, makes a number of interesting points on this subject. He reports the findings of a survey carried out by the Belorussian Komsomol : 'young people read virtually no political material [in the Komsomol press] owing to "its schematic, stereotyped tone and rectilinear conclusions" '.[69] The trouble was that the authorities were 'conducting an internal dispute with their Western opponent, with Soviet readers left in the dark as to the meaning of the dispute, since they had not set eyes on the necessary information in the Western press'.[70] The survey also found that young people were listening to foreign radio programmes to seek 'new facts and information about Soviet life'.

All the same, it is apparent that any change has to be forced grudgingly out of Komsomol leaders, that the Komsomol is reacting to popular need rather than initiating reform. As the once 'angry young man', the poet Yevgeny Yevtushenko has said about the arts and literature, 'Many . . . may be proud that they did not receive the reform and the turn towards openness as a gift from on high. They worked many long years, despite misunderstandings and unjust criticism, to pave the way for the great historic changes.'[71]

The same may be said of many Soviet young people, including more than a few honest Komsomol officials.

Membership

One of the keenest disputes over the Komsomol's future has centred on membership. How many young people would join if they knew non-membership would not harm their career? Should the Komsomol revert to its earlier form of being a small, vanguard group?

The 'numbers game' of enlisting everyone has led to 'indiscriminate acceptance of all and sundry', making youth organisations a 'conveyor belt from the Octobrists [7–9 year olds] to the Pioneers and on to the Komsomol'.[72]

Komsomol secretaries have been judged on the basis of plan fulfilment in terms of membership and have been sacked 'if the number of members does not meet the target set on high'.[73] The system has invariably led to inflation of figures, so that the Leningrad Komsomol recently discovered it had far fewer groups and members than the records showed. How did that happen? 'Up top they demanded good accounts, so we "improved" upon them.'[74] What this means is that 'for years the Komsomol has been too concerned with book-keeping on young people and not with young people themselves'.[75] So what is now sarcastically referred to as the 'multi-million Komsomol army' is not what the figures reveal it to be; nor are its members all enthusiastic young communists.

Indeed, many would not join at all if they had a choice. A survey of Moscow University's biology faculty showed that two-thirds of the students would not have joined the Komsomol if they had known that their careers did not depend on it. What is more, three-quarters felt that during their time in the organisation their civic commitment had either declined or remained static.[76] A Moscow college similarly found that 'the overwhelming majority of students would leave the Komsomol if it would have no adverse effects for them'.[77] But, as a student, Larissa, points out, 'I have no mutual friends in the Komsomol in terms of interests or ideas, there's no one to keep me in. But I won't leave until I'm 28. It's easy for them to get you in, but you can't get out without trouble, and I don't want scandal or trouble.'[78].

The problem for students, as mentioned above, is that a Komsomol reference is generally required for applicants to higher education. And as a young student attests, 'you can't enter some university faculties without being a Komsomol member'.[79] A teacher puts the problem in perspective, 'Preference is at present being given to Komsomol members for entry into higher education. It is no secret that this leads only to mass Komsomol membership by young people in their final year at school ... And with hand on heart I can't say I blame them.'[80] In a survey of five Moscow institutes in 1988, it was found that only 3 per cent of first-year students were outside the Komsomol.[81] A frank criticism of suffocating Party control of the Komsomol by some of the youth organisation's top officials also cited a major reason for the steep rise in the number of independent youth groups as being 'the unwritten law that students must be in the Komsomol ... young people want to be independent.'[82]

The problem does not stop at student entry. Once students are admitted to college, the Komsomol exercises considerable power over them: over the size of their grant, their assessment, their chances of completng their education, their vacation activities, and their career prospects.

The main thrust of widespread criticism is to put a stop to such Komsomol interference in a young person's career: 'Membership of the Komsomol should bring no privileges in being accepted for a college or job.'[83] Partly in response to student criticism and resistance to Komsomol *diktat*, a resolution was passed in October 1987 to establish elected student councils to run student affairs and represent student interests in college and university. They are to be one of three groups (the other two are the Komsomol and the trade unions) involved in student representation[84]

As far as Komsomol membership is concerned, many wish to move away from 'formal admission leading to formal membership', raise the entry age from 14 to 16, introduce a two-year probation period and take only the 'most worthy'.[85] One Moscow student recalls the 1903 dispute between Bolsheviks and Mensheviks over Party membership: 'Yet now the Komsomol is full of people who are just sympathisers, just pay their dues. Do we really need such persons?'[86]

The implications of the debate on Komsomol membership are far-reaching, for if a 'flushing out rather than a purge' is needed, as one young worker suggests,[87] it would surely mean *only about a fifth or less of present members staying in*; and the Komsomol would relinquish its hold over the majority of young people. On the other hand, making membership genuinely voluntary and open to the dedicated might be the only way the Komsomol can begin to recover respect and authority.

In any case, the Komsomol has lost its monopoly as the country's only youth organisation. As its own monthly journal says, 'it has lost the initiative in influencing a substantial number of young men and women'.[88] With many young people preferring membership of an informal club, some Komsomol members have proposed that the Komsomol should play down political indoctrination, labour recruitment, military and patriotic training, and focus more on interest groups – in sport, music, literature, drama. One radical proposal at the 20th Komsomol Congress was that it should become merely a leisure group for young people.[89] Of course, that would mean it losing many members, 'but that only scares those pseudo-Komsomol members who joined because they had to, like everyone else'.[90]

There are those Komsomol leaders who call for the organisation to make use of the 'street leaders' of the informal clubs, since they clearly enjoy more respect among young people than the Komsomol secretaries do.[91] To some in authority this may seem the only way of regaining control over Soviet youth; to others it may seem a genuine attempt at 'power-sharing', at giving youth something of what they want, rather than what the Party and Komsomol think they ought to want and have. Ignored for so long, however, many young men and women may well feel it is too late even for that.

POST-CONGRESS DEVELOPMENTS

The 20th Komsomol Congress, held between 15 and 19 April 1987, had been heralded as the forum that would begin to right the above-mentioned failings and bring about the rebirth of the Komsomol. The Congress heard two major speeches, one from Gorbachov, who arrived with the entire Party Politburo, but who used the youth forum to address the world, not specifically Soviet youth, and one from Mironenko, who took up four and a half pages of *Komsomolskaya pravda* with a frank admission of past errors and intentions to do better.[92] All the same, the Party-donated slate of candidates for the 334-member Central Committee exactly fitted available places and evidently went through 'on the nod'.

While Mironenko studiously avoided mention of the Komsomol's present membership, he stressed the need for a strictly vountary, individual acceptance of all future members; he also made references to enhancement of the powers of local Komsomol branches and an end to undue interference in their affairs from above. While making no mention of any relinquishing of the Komsomol's monopoly of either youth organisations or youth literature, he made a fierce attack on religion and indifference to atheism, on the one hand, and 'commercial bourgeois products and home-grown vulgar pop songs', on the other.

Mironenko reported on the dwindling financial resources (evidently a new Party policy towards the Komsomol to force it to put its house in order) that were insufficient to maintain its 350 000 full-time staff, 49 colleges, 33 museums, seven propaganda trains, 30 youth camps, three publishing houses, 15 youth palaces and five Pioneer camps.[93] It was later reported that revenue had increased 4.5 times in recent years, but expenditure has increased six times. So the Komsomol was now in debt and had to cut its staff; as many as 56 of the 86 territorial, regional and Republican Komsomol organisations were only surviving through subsidies which were gradually to be removed so that all Komsomol branches would be self-financing.[94]

Of considerable interest were the new Komsomol rules (*Ustav*), which superseded those adopted by the 16th Congress in 1970. The new rules included some 100 amendments as a result of pre-Congress discussion (though thousands were rejected; of the Leningrad delegations's 202 proposed amendments, for example, only two were adopted[95]) and produced two opposing votes and four abstentions (not reported in the Komsomol press) – the first time such a daring action had been made since the mid-1920s.[96]

The new rules contain some interesting changes. First, from being 'a social organisation embracing the wide mass of progressive youth', the Komsomol is now defined as 'a socio-*political* organisation embracing the *advanced section* of youth', and the rules cite Lenin's recommendation that the Komsomol should be a 'shock group' [authors italics]. This is a return to the early definition.[97]

Secondly, while the age parameters remain the same (14–28), much emphasis is now put on the individual and voluntary nature of membership, on secret voting and on the nomination of any number of candidates who must be open to scrutiny and criticism at all levels (Article 15). Thirdly, a whole new section 'the Komsomol and State and Republic Organisations' has been added to the Rules, indicating a desire to return the Komsomol to the more active, independent role in the country's affairs it had had in the early 1920s, and stressing its need to possess legislative initiative on behalf of youth interests.

It will be interesting to see how soon and how much of the new rule book will become reality. One major implication would seem to be that young people will no longer have to join in order to get on, except in politics. All the same, for many young people, including Komsomol officials, the Congress was a 'damp squib', as irrelevant to youth needs as are Vatican pontifications to Western youth. When *Sobesednik* invited readers to give their impressions of the Congress, it did not receive a single letter and devoted two pages to analysing the reasons why.[98]

SOME CONCLUDING THOUGHTS

1. The Komsomol was born in the midst of war, when the very survival of the communist government was in the balance. The shape it took in the formative years reflected the exigencies of war. Once the war was over and the country turned to recovery, then rapid industrialisation and collectivisation of farming, Stalin's 'revolutionary imperative' made a virtue out of necessity of the wartime Komsomol role and structure, stamping its imprint on the Komsomol. Seventy years on from revolution, conditions are radically different; yet the Komsomol is still basically cast in the mould that the Civil War and Stalin forced it into.

To fully appreciate the need for change, Komsomol leaders need to review Komsomol history. And this appears to be what they are doing. As Victor Mironenko has said recently, 'Let us turn once more to the history of our own League. Let us study it so that we can better understand the present, more profoundly appreciate the measure of our responsibility for the future of the country and the Komsomol.'[99]

2. We clearly have to make a distinction between the effectiveness of the Octobrists and Pioneers, on the one hand, and that of the Komsomol on the other, between the *voluntary* nature of Pioneer activities and the 'ritual participation', or what Unger has called the 'voluntary compulsion', of the Komsomol involvement with young people.[100] There seems to be a cut-off point about the age of 15 at which the youth movement's influence diminishes sharply. It may have integrated some young people into building a socialist society, but it has clearly estranged others through excessive bureaucracy,

discipline, routine and invasions of personal lifestyles. Times are changing and the Komsomol is slow to adapt; it is hard to maintain revolutionary enthusiasm among girls and boys born in the 1970s. Nor is it easy to bring up young people in what they perceive as old-fashioned, parochial values at a time when increasing exposure to Western youth culture and the growing restlessness of urban teen-agers are leading to a polarisation of values between the younger and older generations. Established youth organisations and the church are encountering similar problems in the West.

3. In criticising the Komsomol it is easy to lose sight of the positive role it has played over the years, and continues to play even today. It has historically played a part in the political socialisation of young people, in developing the values and skills appropriate to a modern-ising economy, in acting as a new socialising agency in a period when rapid social transformation was eroding the traditional foundation of socialisation – through the family, kinship groups, local community and religious organisations – and in creating the cultured, hard-working and honest personality who aspires to live up to the ideals of the 'new Soviet person'. In school the youth organisations would seem to have been powerful back-up forces to teachers in encourag-ing diligence, discipline and selflessness, which are probably all the more effective coming from the peer group itself rather than being imposed by adults (though it is adults that ultimately set the stand-ards).

Any assessment of the historical role of the Komsomol, therefore, has to be measured at least in part against these considerations.

4. One of the inevitable consequences of the Komsomol being the only permitted youth organisation of the only permitted Party in power is the spawning within it of 'bandwagon' careerists, corrupt officials, political 'radishes' (red on the outside, white on the inside) who pay lip service to communism and concern for young people, while enjoying their *frais de représéntation*: trips abroad, chauffeur-driven limousines, special (closed to the public) shops, hospitals, dachas, rest homes, their high salaries augmented by their large tax-free 'packet', their private film screenings, their booked seats in top theatres (sometimes for whole performances), and the rest. Such a blatant abuse of privileges, the dividends of political rank developed since Lenin's death, have helped create a bureaucracy of privileged Komsomol functionaries divorced from real life, from young people, their needs and interests, intent on preserving their own position. Such bureaucrats have risen, moreover, not by the will and demands

of those beneath them, but by appointment from above, from Party officials on whom they are entirely dependent.

This anti-Leninist , antithetical to communism, system of privileges has long since destroyed any popular belief that young people are masters of their own country and destiny. It has blunted the feeling of responsibility for what happens around them, it has created a 'them v us' syndrome where 'they' enjoy perquisites gained not from owning property or from class exploitation, but from *control* over the fruits of others' labour, from privileges abrogated by the ruling Party and its youth oroganisation. 'We' respond in varying degrees of passivity, resignation and, in recent years, active resistance, partly motivated by disillusionment from a socialist viewpoint with insincere moral-isers and cynical careerists.

It is clearly not going to be easy to curb the careerists and convince Soviet youth that their political leaders are making a genuine attempt to establish real socialists values – or, indeed, any honest values, since in the eyes of many young people, 'socialism' has been badly tarnished by the 'pseudo-socialism' of some of its practitioners.

5. If young people are to feel that they are being listened to and trusted, the Komsomol (and Party) will have to accept many far-reaching and profound changes in the old ways of governing. Gorbachov has spelled out what he means by 'overhauling the present state of affairs': 'Above all, more trust in young people . . . more independence to them in their work, studies, daily life and leisure, and more responsibility for their actions. All this presupposes the right for them to take part in governing society at all levels.[101]

We shall see. It will not be enough for the Komsomol to adapt methods, structure and personnel in order to regain control. It has sincerely to abide by Lenin's principle of giving young people complete independence, complete freedom from Komsomol tutel-age. Young people need to feel trusted (even to travel abroad without having first to provide their political loyalty and fitness in the Komsomol). Without that, no amount of tinkering with structural procedures, membership and methods will produce the desired effect.

For change is not coming about as a gift from above; it has been fought for courageously and often dangerously by young people, frequently much maligned, over a number of years. And they will not now forfeit their gains or put at risk the hopeful prospects offered by the reforms without a struggle. In that struggle the Komsomol will have to decide which side it is on.

Notes

1. Lenin, V. I., 'Internatsional molodyozhi', *Polnoye sobranie sochineniy*, vol. 30 (Moscow: Progress, 1975) p. 226. A student at Moscow's Maurice Thorez Foreign Languages Institute was disciplined by the Party, accused of trying to drive a wedge between the Party and Komsomol, and of distorting Lenin precisely for quoting this passage in the Komsomol wall newspaper (see *Sobesednik* June 1987, no. 24 p. 3). Interestingly, the passage was published in *Sobesednik*, without comment, two months later (see *Sobesednik*, August 1987, no. 33, p. 3).
2. Ibid. vol. 8, p. 124.
3. *Kommunisticheskaya partiya Sovetskovo Soyuza v rezolyutsiakh i resheniyakh syezdov, konferentsiy i plenumov TsK, 1898–1954*, 7th edn, Part I (Moscow: Politizdat, 1954) p. 386. The resolution was reprinted in *Sobesednik* in March 1987, no. 12, p. 2.
4. *Pervy vserossiysky syezd RKSM*, 3rd edn, (Moscow-Leningrad: Molodaya gvardia, 1926) p. 98.
5. Ibid., pp. 197–8.
6. Fisher, Ralph, *Pattern for Soviet Youth. A Study of the Congresses of the Komsomol, 1918–1954* (New York: Columbia University Press, 1959) p. 141.
7. Ibid., p. 28. Party membership at the time of the Third Komsomol Congress was 600 000 – see *Tretiy vserossiysky syezd rossiyskovo kommunisticheskovo soyuza molodyozhi* (Moscow–Leningrad: Molodaya gvardia, 1926) p. 28.
8. *VII syezd vsesoyuznovo leninskovo kommunisticheskovo soyuza molodyozhi* (Moscow–Leningrad: Molodaya gvardia, 1926) p. 193.
9. *VKP (b) o komsomole i molodyozhi. Sbornik resheniy i postanovleniy partii o molodyozhi (1903–1938)* (Moscow: Molodaya gvardia, 1938) p. 77.
10. 'At a closed Komsomol meeting members conduct accounts and election of the committee, the bureau and secretary, and discuss the personal affairs of members' (see *Organizatsionno-ustavnye voprosy Komsomolskoi raboty* (Moscow: Molodaya gvardia, 1973, p. 40).
11. 'Members of the Komsomol attaining the age of 28 cease to be members unless they are chosen for leading Komsomol posts' (see *Ustav vsesoyuznovo leninskovo kommunisticheskovo soyuza molodyozhi* (Moscow: Molodaya gvardia, 1985, p. 10).
12. *Vsesoyuzny leninsky kommunistichesky soyuz molodyozhi. Naglyadnoye posobie* (Moscow: Molodoya gvardia, 1985) p. 67.
13. *Sobesednik*, March 1987, no. 13, p. 4.
14. See 'Ustav Vsesoyuznovo leninskovo kommunisticheskovo soyuza molodyozhi utverzhden XX syezdom VLKSM', *Komsomolskaya pravda*, 21 April 1987, p. 93.
15. *Ustav vsesoyuznovo leninskovo kommunisticheskovo soyuza molodyozhi* (Moscow: Molodoya gvardia, 1985) p. 10.
16. *Organizatsionno-ustavnye voprosy Komsomolskoi raboty*, p. 59.
17. Ibid., p. 58.

18. Oddly, *Soviet Weekly* (28 February, p. 3) gave 42m in February 1987 and 40m in April (25 April, p. 1). In January, *Molodoi kommunist* (1987, no. 1, p. 17) put membership at 42m; in October this was reduced to 40.8m (1987, no. 10, p. 52).

19. See Fisher, *Pattern for Soviet Youth* (note 6) p. 280; *VLKSM Naglyadnoye posobie*, p. 29; *Molodoi kommunist*, 1987, no. 3, p. 9.

20. *VLKSM Naglyadnoye posobie* (note 12), p. 5.

21. Bagandov, B. M., *Obshchestvenno-politicheskoye vospitanie starsheklassnikov* (Moscow: Molodoya gvardia, 1982) p. 83.

22. 'Sulemov, V. A., (ed.), *Istoriya VLKSM i Vsesoyuznoi pionerskoi organizatsii imeni V. I. Lenina* (Moscow: Prosveshchenie, 1983, p. 5).

23. Mironenko, V., 'Every person is unique,' *Sport in the USSR*, 1988, no. 3, p. 10.

24. Fisher, *Pattern for Soviet Youth* (note 6), p. 280; *Narodnoye khozyaistvo SSSR v 1955 g* (Moscow: Statistika, 1956, p. 17).

25. *VLKSM Naglyadnoye posobie* (note 12), pp. 33–4; *Narodnoye khozyaistvo SSSR v 1985 g* (Moscow: statistika, 1986, p. 15).

26. *Molodoi kommunist*, 1987, no. 10, p. 52.

27. Fisher, *Pattern for Soviet Youth* (note 6), p. 280; *VLKSM Naglyadnoye posobie*, p. 48; *Zhenshchiny i deti v SSSR* (Moscow: Finansy i Statistika, 1985, p. 28); *Soviet Weekly*, 28 November 1987, p. 10.

28. *VLKSM Naglyadnoye posobie* (note 12), p. 135.

29. *Pravda*, 7 July 1984, p. 2.

30. Gorbachov, M. S., 'O perestroike i kadrovoi politike partii', *Izvestiya*, 28 January 1987, p. 2.

31. Fisher, *Pattern for Soviet Youth* (note 6), p. 280.

32. *VLKSM Naglyadnoye posobie* (note 12), p. 45.

33. Ibid., p. 141.

34. Fisher, *Pattern for Soviet Youth* (note 6), p. 282.

35. *VLKSM Naglyadnoye posobie* (note 12), pp. 49–50.

36. Ibid., pp. 135–6.

37. See *Molodoi kommunist*, 1986, no. 6, p. 16.

38. Petukhov, S., 'Khvataemsya za vse', *Sobesednik*, January 1987, no. 5, p. 2.

39. Petrovichev, N. A., *Vazhny faktor vozrastaniya rukovodyashchei roli KPSS* (Moscow: Politizdat, 1979) p. 147; see also *Molodoi kommunist*, 1987, no. 10, p. 53.

40. *Vstupayushchemu v Komsomol* (Moscow: Molodoya gvardia, 1976, p. 35).

41. Khose, S. Y., *Uchitelskaya komsomolskaya organizatsiya* (Moscow: Prosveshchenie, 1983, p. 8).

42. See *Moscow News*, 1987, no. 13, p. 8.

43. Personal communication in Leningrad.

44. See *Sotsiologicheskie issledovaniya*, 1987, no. 1, p. 95.

45. Vladimir Klyuev, 'My redko sovershaem smelye postupki', *Sobesednik*, August 1987, no. 32, p. 4.

46. Victor Mironenko, 'Zavetnye stranitsy', *Sobesednik*, February 1987, no. 6, p. 3.

47. Ilvnsky, Igor, 'Perestroika sostoitsya yesli...' *Molodoi kommunist*, no. 12, 1987, p. 13.

48. 'Nam ne nuzhny v komsomole "prozasedavshiesya"', *Sobesednik*, September 1986, no. 38, p. 4.

49. Ibid.

50. *Pravda*, 3 February 1986, p. 3. It was this critical letter that the Party's ideology chief, Yegor Ligachov, condemned, saying that *Pravda* had gone beyond reasonable limits in its discussion of high privilege – see *Pravda*, 28 February 1986, p. 1.

51. Yakovlev, A., *Sobesednik*, September 1986, no. 38, p. 4.

52. Igor Chernyak, 'Za dvoinoi dveryu', *Sobesednik*, January 1987, no. 4, p. 4.

53. Nozhin, Y., 'Ne prinimayut slovo', *Molodoi kommunist*, 1984, no. 8, p. 28.

54. Pavel Gusev, 'Shtoby chitatel nam veril', *Molodoi kommunist*, 1987, no. 5, p. 35.

55. See *Molodoi kommunist*, 1987, no. 5, p. 59.

56. Pronina, Y., 'Sobranie dlya galochki', *Molodoi kommunist*, 1986, no. 12, p. 30.

57. Kononova, N., 'Ne naznachat – vybirat!' *Sobesednik*, January 1987, no. 5, p. 2.

58. *Sovetsky soyuz*, 1987, no. 5, pp. 6–8.

59. Kononova, 'Ne naznachat ...! (note 57), p. 2.

60. Podebry, O., 'Razvedka delom', *Sobesednik*, November 1986, no. 45, p. 2.

61. Ufimtsev, A., 'Na ravnykh', *Sobesednik*, January 1987, no. 5, p. 2.

62. Podebry, 'Razvedta delom' (note 60), p. 2.

63. See *Komsomolskaya pravda*, 3 November 1985, p. 1.

64. Bovrik, V. S., and Mukhachov, V. I., 'Obshchestvenno-politicheskaya aktivnost molodyozhi', in Cherednichenko, G. A., and Shubkin, V. N., *Molodyozh vstupaet v zhizn* (Moscow: Prosveshchenie, 1985, p. 114).

65. See Kharchev, A. G., and Alexeyeva, V. G., *Obraz zhizni. Moral. Vospitanie* (Moscow: Izdatelstvo politicheskoi literatury, 1977) p. 70.

66. Malikova, S., 'Neuzheli i vezde tak zhe?' *Molodoi kommunist*, 1987, no. 12, p. 98.

67. Filipenko, Y., 'The Komsomol goes back to the people', *Soviet Weekly*, 28 November 1987, p. 10.

68. Kagarlitsky, B., 'The intelligentsia and the changes', *New Left Review*, 1987, no. 164, pp. 18–19.

69. Dragovets, V., 'Oruzhiem pravdy i ubezhdeniya', *Molodoi kommunist*, 1987, no. 1, p. 15. There have been many complaints that young people no longer read the Soviet press, including from Archbishop Mikhail of Vologda and Velikoustyug – see *Pravda*, 21 December 1987, p. 2.

70. Dragovets, 'Oruzheim pravda' (note 69), pp. 15–17.

71. Yevtushenko, Y., 'The right to be unconventional', *Soviet Weekly*, 14 February 1987, p. 13.

72. Rotar, P., *Sobesednik*, January 1987, no. 5, p. 2.

73. Movergoz, V., 'Komu platit zarplatu?' *Sobesednik*, Janury 1987, no. 5, p. 2.
74. 'Printsipialno, bez kompromissov', *Sobesednik*, December 1986, no. 51, p. 2.
75. Kuklin, A., 'Legko li stat vzroslym', *Sobesednik*, February 1987, no. 6, p. 12.
76. 'Ne po ankete – po prizvaniyu', *Sobesednik*, December 1986, no. 49, p. 2.
77. Larissa, S., 'Sverim ryady', *Sobesednik*, December 1986, no. 50, p. 11.
78. Ibid.
79. Levin, V., 'Privilegiya odna – byt vperedi!' *Sobesednik*, January 1987, no. 3, p. 2.
80. Klenitskaya, I., 'Bez planov rosta,' *Sobesednik*, February 1987, no. 7, p. 2.
81. Poleshchuk, A., 'Ask Andrei,' *Soviet Weekly*, 5 March 1988, p. 7.
82. Sibirev, N., 'Doverie? Polnoye!' *Sobesednik*, June 1988, no. 24, pp. 4–5.
83. 'Ne po ankete . . .' *Sobesednik*, December 1986, no. 49, p. 2.
84. 'Gorizont dlya studsoveta', *Sobesednik*, September 1987, no. 37, p. 13.
85. See *Sobesednik*, no. 29, p. 10; no. 36, p. 4; no. 38, p. 5; no. 49, p. 2 – all for 1986.
86. Ugrekhelidze, V., *Sobesednik*, September 1986, no. 38, p. 5.
87. Martynenko, O., *Sobesednik*, September 1986, no. 38, p. 5.
88. Kulikov, V., 'Gomo NOMO zhdyot vnimaniya', *Molodoi kommunist*, 1986, no. 12, p. 25.
89. Bokiya, S., 'XX syezd VLKSM, aktivizatsiya sistemy komsomolskoi politicheskoi seti', Speech given in May 1987 at the Leningrad Dom Politicheskovo Prosveshcheniya.
90. Yakovlev, A., *Sobesednik*, September 1986, no. 38, p. 4.
91. 'Printsipialno, bez kompromissov', *Sobesednik*, December 1986, no. 51, p. 2.
92. 'Otchot TsK VLKSM i zadachi Komsomola po dalneishemu usileniyu kommunisticheskovo vospitaniya molodyozhi v svete ustanovok XXVII syezda KPSS. Oklad pervovo sekretarya TsK VLKSM V.Mironenko', *momsomolskaya pravda*, 16 April 1987, pp. 2–7.
93. Sokolov, M., 'Nashe vremya, nashi dengi', *Sobesednik*, 1987, no. 46, p. 3.
94. Ibid., p. 5. See also *Molodoi kommunist*, 1987, No. 10, p. 5, and *Argumenty i fakty*, August 1987.
95. Personal communication.
96. See 'Youth put peace first', *Soviet Weekly*, 25 April 1987, p. 1. Neither *Komsomolskaya pravda*, nor *Pravda*, nor *Molodoi kommunist* made mention of this dissention.'
97. 'Ustav Vsesoyuznovo Leninskovo Kommunisticheskovo Soyuza Molodyozhi utverzhdyon XX syezdom VLKSM', *Komsomolskaya pravda*, 21 April 1987, pp. 2–3.
98. Lukov, V., 'Sevodnya ili nikogda!' *Sobesdnik*, July 1987, no. 27, pp. 4–5.

99. Mironenko, V., 'Zavetnye stranitsy', Sobesednik, February 1987, no. 6, p. 3.
100. See Unger, Aryeh, 'Political participation in the USSR: YCL and CPSU', *Soviet Studies*, vol. 33, no. 1, January 1981, p. 111.
101. Gorbachov, M. S., 'Doklad na plenume TsK KPSS: O perestroike i kadrovoi politike partii', *Izvestiya*, 28 January 1987, p. 2.

3 The Rock Music Community
Paul Easton

> Any musical innovation is full of danger to the whole State, and
> ought to be prohibited; when modes of music change, the funda-
> mental laws of the State always change with them.
>
> *Plato*, The Republic, *Book IV*

INTRODUCTION

The speed and depth of change that has taken place in the world of
non-professional Soviet pop and rock music since the summer of 1986
has been little short of staggering. The Soviet authorities, after years
of deriding rock as a bourgeois, decadent genre, after years of
attempting either to suppress or dilute the unofficial rock community,
have come to realise that *perestroika* demands an accommodation
with youth. In order to put what follows in perspective, a history of
the rock music movement in the USSR begins this chapter; the
second section deals with attitudes and lifestyles of the rock community. Finally the treatment of the rock community since the
accession of M. S. Gorbachov to Party leadership in March 1985 is
looked at in more detail and the motives behind the new policies and
possible consequences are examined.

. *Glasnost* has provided an abundance of Soviet material on youth
affairs. Such films as *It Isn't Easy to be Young*, made in the Riga Film
Studios, have shown the reality of Soviet youth in a way never before
attempted. The monolithic uniformity of young people in the Soviet
Union that had hitherto been portrayed in the West and, to some
extent, strived for by Soviet policy has been inaccurate probably for
many years. Drug taking, gang violence, heavy metal and other 'evils'
may be new to the pages of *Komsomolskaya pravda* and other
publications, but they are far from new to youth who have been
engaging in these activities for some time.

This chapter is about one section, albeit very sizeable, of Soviet
youth and does not attempt to represent youth as a whole. By the

rock music community is meant those young people who write, play and listen to what is now called 'amateur rock music'. This is the music that was once referred to as 'underground', and although amateur may be a misnomer, it refers to non-professional status rather than content; the use of the word 'underground' has long been outdated. As explained below, attempts to eradicate the rock movement were soon replaced by moves to control it, which meant rock groups and the State were brought into a relationship that gave official recognition to this amateur movement.

The rock community is not defined merely by a love of rock music. It is the shared lifestyles and philosophies that really unite it. That these are so far removed from those desirable in the ideal New Soviet Person is not surprising. Even that great bulk of Soviet youth that realises advancement is based upon conformity pays only lip service to these values.[1] What is surprising is that the rock community has become a *cause célèbre* in the media in recent times, most comment being highly favourable. A commentator in *Literaturnaya gazeta* even went so far as to suggest that 'rock has created the aesthetics of daily living (*byt*)'.[2]

Soviet rock differs most fundamentally from the Western original in the stress put upon the lyrics. The lyrics express the attitudes and philosophy of the rock community and are its litany. I have therefore made use of extended quotes from songs. Difficulties in translation make some of them sound fairly banal and the reader is asked to concentrate on the message they convey rather than their 'poetic' value.

Much of the information for this chapter comes from interviews I have carried out with members of the rock community, some formal, some informal. Over the last two years I have spent much time in the USSR, mainly in Leningrad, and have become friendly with many members of the rock community, especially the musicians themselves. I have been to many concerts, listened to much of the music, and, as far as possible, lived with the rock community. Much of this chapter is based upon what I perceive to be the collective attitudes of the rock community.

HISTORY OF THE ROCK COMMUNITY

Rock and roll music began in the West in the late 1950s with such singers as Chuck Berry. Almost at once it was condemned by the older generation as being wild, erotic and anti-social. The same had been said thirty years before with regard to jazz, of which rock and roll was a descendent. Jazz had also been a subject for much discussion in the Soviet Union. Indeed for a few months in 1927 *Izvestiya*, and *Pravda* argued over the merits of this new musical genre. In the end, *Pravda* won the day, arguing that this was the music of the oppressed Southern American Negros, and jazz became an accepted feature of Soviet culture (albeit with periods of repression).[3]

The timing of the beginning of pop music in the West helps to explain how quickly it achieved popularity in the Soviet Union. At the end of the 1950s, trade and cultural links expanded greatly as a result of a lull in the cold war. Foreigners brought pop records, newspapers and magazines into the USSR. Although at first such items were mainly intended as gifts for friends, pop paraphernalia rapidly became a growth area on the black market. Naturally, pop fans were mostly confined to those big European cities in which contacts with foreigners were most frequent, such as Moscow, Leningrad, Tallin, Riga and Lvov. But right from the start pop music attracted a wide audience. As a Soviet rock critic has written,

> The demand for pop recordings ... at the beginning of the sixties was already enormous, while record and tape supplies were in catastrophically short supply. This led to the birth of a legendary phenomenon – the memorable records 'on ribs' ... They were actually X-ray plates (chest cavities, spinal cords, broken bones) rounded at the edge with scissors, with a small hole in the centre and grooves that were barely visible on the surface. Such an extravagant choice of raw material for these 'flexidiscs' is easily explained: X-ray plates were the cheapest and most readily available source of necessary plastic. People bought them by the hundreds from hospitals and clinics for kopeks, after which grooves were cut with the help of special machines (made, they say, from old records by skilled conspiratorial hands). The 'ribs' were marketed, naturally, under the table. The quality was awful, but the price was low, a ruble or a ruble and a half.[4]

This demand was small, however, compared to that which occurred in the late 1960s when the Beatles entered their hippy/Buddhist stage. 'The majority of Russian youth was set alight by the mixture of anarchy and collectivism which they felt the Beatles represented ... They became for the Soviets not only musical but spiritual leaders.'[5] The first Soviet pop groups came into existence at once. In the spring of 1963 the first Beatles album came out and already by December the Leningrad group *Stranniki* (Wanderers) equipped with D-I-Y guitars, had given their first concert.[6]

At first the groups had done little more than sing poor imitations of the Beatles in English. But now they began to copy the example rather than the songs of the Beatles and wrote their own compositions. The Beatles style 'accorded well with the Russian view that worthwhile music only comes from a group; individual composers have little credit'.[7] The Soviet music industry was nevertheless based on the precept that composing was the prerogative of individual professionals, memebrs of the Composers Union. Freddie Starr writes that as a result of this new trend, 'for the first time the government's seemingly unshakeable monopoly on the "Soviet tin pan alley" was challenged'.[8]

Pop music grew rapidly in popularity.

In 1969 it was estimated that there was not a high school, institute or factory in Moscow without at least one rock band, bringing the total to several thousand and meaning that several thousand private and independent producers were operating in the field of popular culture. No party at Moscow State University was complete without rock music and even the Komsomol was wholly dependent on the private market when it hired music for its dances.[9]

This uncontrolled movement was not to stay that way for long. The first official move came in response to a 'scandalous' concert in Leningrad in 1967.

One of the most popular bands, the Argonauts, had been engaged to play at the Polytechnic Institute. The hall was packed with students and rock fans among whom word had spread that this was to be a wild evening. The fans drank vodka in the hall, and many got high on marijuana. When the Argonauts performed a few fans attacked the stage and began shouting and attacking the musicians ... A special session of the city Central Committee of the Communist Party was held and a decree issued asserting public control over all vocal guitar bands in Leningrad. Amateur groups were prevented from appearing in public until they had gained permission from the House of People's Creativity on Rubinstein Street. The Leningrad Artistic Council was made directly accountable to the local Party.[10]

The natural inclination of the authorities to control and suppress rock was not based purely on grounds of maintaining public order. Ideologically it was seen as a bourgeois, decadent genre that represented the decay in capitalist countries. Such a thesis conveniently ignored the fact that much of the Western rock movement revolved around protest at this very decay. All kinds of justifications were made to support this official attitude with one commentator going so far as to suggest that rock music in Russian was 'an impossibility on account of the specific rhythmical structure of the Russian language'.[11]

Such energies expended on suppressing pop music in those days might have been premature. The apathy, distrust of authority and muted anarchy typical of the 1980s were far from widespread at the start of the 1970s. Song lyrics concerned themselves primarily with the 'boy meets girl and falls in love' theme. As a Soviet *émigré* has written, 'While Soviet youth in those days was very interested in Western counter-culture and the "youth revolution", its own conflict went no further than an adolescent rebellion marked by the playing of electric guitars. This rather backward attitude was linked to the prevailing atmosphere of faith in Communism and the belief that universal happiness and self-fulfilment were just around the corner.'[12]

As a response to the demand for Western-style music, the authorities began in 1969 to set up officially approved bands which they designated as 'vocal/instrumental ensembles' (VIAs). These groups, unlike the 'amateurs', 'played songs by members of the Union of Composers, and their stage appearances were strictly regulated by "artistic committees" consisting of Party officials, censors and ideological guardians'.[13] They were able to gain much popularity, especially in provincial towns where there were then no alternatives. In content they were little different from the amateurs, but their technical advantages (their equipment was provided by the state), and greater opportunities to perform meant that they were soon of much greater significance than the amateurs. The second half of the 1970s produced changes, however, that dramatically altered the situation.

The stagnation, decay and corruption of the Brezhnev era that effectively began in the mid-1960s brought much disillusionment to Soviet young people. The gap between official interpretations of society and reality had become so wide that young people could no longer stretch their credulity to the extent that the previous generation had. This had its effect on the rock and pop scene:

The sweet dream of Soviet romanticism in political and public life as in the pop scene had played itself out. The generation of the

1960s had got married and either abandoned music altogether or joined the ranks of the state's musical hirelings. They were replaced by a new breed, a generation who were bitter and anxious and much more independent than their predecessors.[14]

This new generation, having lost faith in the Soviet leadership, sought out new leaders and, as in the West, many turned to rock musicians for spiritual guidance in a society widely perceived as lacking in morality. Such a leader was Boris Grebenshchikov, leader and songwriter of the group Aquarium which is probably the most famous and enduring group on the Soviet rock scene. Boris's communal appartment on Ulitsa Sofia Peresofa in Leningrad bears witness to the kind of emotions inspired by these 'custodians' of the popular conscience. The stairwell leading up to his flat on the eighth floor is literally covered with graffiti. 'Boris, you are life'. 'We cannot survive without you.' 'Aquarium – the mind and conscience of Soviet youth' (a parody of a famous Lenin poster). Although these may seem to be just the emotional expressions of isolated hippies, it is the place-names beneath these scrawls that are most revealing: Novosibirsk, Kiev and numerous other towns thousands of miles away. Climbing the stairs, one is bound to meet at least one young girl or boy sitting patiently, waiting for Boris to appear. Etiquette demands that they do not pass the fifth floor. Many have travelled long distances just to feel his hand on theirs. There seems to be something religious about such pilgrimages; indeed Boris's commitment to Christianity is well-known and features in his lyrics. Only John Lennon commands more respect and, since his death, he has become a near Christ-like figure to Soviet hippies.

Aquarium was formed in 1975 and, along with the group Time Machine from Moscow, was first to achieve 'supergroup' status in the Soviet Union. Aquarium sings about many themes: love and estrangement, disappointed expectations, stories of Chinese philosophers, even a Russian equivalent of Irish folk ditties. Sometimes their language is esoteric and hard to understand, at other times blatantly transparent. Boris is also concerned at the loss of individuality in Soviet society: 'Our lyrics are spiritually orientated. Who am I in relation to power? Do I want to be guided? Who guides me? Who controls me? What is our relationship? Not the boy/girl relationship but the relationship between myself as a person and you as a crowd.'[15] Time Machine came closer to setting the tone that survives into the 1980s through songs about the actual situation of youth, their frustrations and emptiness, portrayed in often cynical and ironic manner. Their lyricist, Andrei Makarevich, demonstrates this cynicism in the song 'Your Birthday':

It's summertime today
Hurrying to send you my wishes,
It's your birthday today
So good luck, good luck . . .

You laid the table long ago
Friends are coming round today
Friends of friends who couldn't
   care less
Come they might, but then might
   not.
Wine will be drunk
The boy by the window will drink
Till he's pissed.
It ain't his wine
And he ain't a hooligan,
He just don't know who you are.
Then someone will suddenly
   decide
That the girl over there

Is a bit of alright. Wouldn't mind
   a woman like her
She doesn't mind a bit of a chat,
But 'course she's soon off home.

So he gives that one a miss.
There'll be nothing but talk
About music and jeans
Not to mention the weather in
   Heaven.
But in the small hours
When friends have long gone
And only the loneliness remains
You're forgotten on the table
Like an old packet of cigarettes.
I'm hurrying to bring you my
   best wishes
I'm hurrying to say Happy
   Birthday
'cos today you're a year older.[16]

A rock fan told me of her response to the new music.

I was 17, studying at college. I'd listened to rock for years on the BBC. I loved the power but couldn't understand the words. When I listened to Aquarium it made a great deal of sense. Rock music with Russian poetry. My friends listened to these new sounds in amazement. We left it to Grebenshchikov to decide what was right or wrong. We didn't believe anyone else. Rock became a way of life.[17]

Certainly in Leningrad and Moscow, where there was some chance of hearing the music, many thousands of young people were assimilating the values and norms of a new culture through the medium of rock music.

Such growth had its negative side. This was a time when the movement was truly 'underground'. Forced into this position, it became simple prey for speculators. Concerts were rarely officially sanctioned and most took place either in private flats or in public auditoria where the custodian either had a plan to storm or an eye to profit. As the numbers involved grew, so did the pickings, *Komsomolskaya pravda* gave a sardonic description of an out-of-town Time Machine concert:

> They agreed to meet early, at 11, an hour before the start. He appeared at the station *65-Kilometres* a few minutes early and began to observe the electric trains spewing crowds of excited, fashionably dressed youths on to the platform one after another. The trains arrived full to bursting and departed almost deserted. Korolyov thought to himself: if each train holds, say, a thousand people and five trains have already come and gone, that makes five thousand people already who had happily purchased tickets. Korolyov multipled five thousand by five rubles and suddenly his friends appeared.[18]

The paper printed a letter explaining the logic of the situation:

> I'm middle-aged, already fifty, but I listened delightedly to the recordings of these groups, which my son had acquired somewhere ... It's a shame that our youth who know about Time Machine can't hear their music. Is it really that we don't have enough concert halls or palaces of culture? And is it right that money which could go to the state purse falls into the thick wallets of speculators and swindlers?[19]

In the same article the paper printed a letter by a reader that was probably more representative of the general public's attitude towards rock. 'It's the police who are guilty. Four thousand wild-haired thugs, providing nourishment for speculators. These people don't know the meaning of a day's work, they worship these modern idols with a herd-instinct. Put a stop to this rock music!'[20] In the end, the authorities preferred the first reader's approach. They had little choice.

At the start of the 1980s a new phenomenon appeared. Groups began to record albums. In small flats with often home-built, two-track recorders, cassettes were produced and album covers designed by the avant-garde art movement. This was the beginning of rock *magnetizdat*, the distribution of sound by cassette. For the first time the music of groups, whose names were only familiar from press condemnation, could be heard by young people throughout the country. It was not long before this phenomenon manifested itself in declining attendances at official concerts of vocal/instrumental ensembles, matched by a fall in the sale of their albums. This was one factor that caused such organisations as *Goskontsert*, the state concert organisation, to hire Time Machine and promote them to professional status. Many groups followed this example, assuming that this move would give them better equipment, wider exposure and the chance to earn a more secure living.

These professional rock groups did achieve success, but in the process lost their original audience. Their lyrics now came under state censorship. Only a song with an official permit to perform could be played. As it was, many bands simply began to censor themselves. The lyrics lost their biting edge. The gruelling schedules of tours took the musicians away from the life they had written about in their songs and the new lyrics were alien to their original fans. Andrei Makarevich expressed his bitterness at the treatment he received in his song 'Barrier' and also raised a rhetorical question that now, in this era of *glasnost*, has a special significance for the rock movement.

> You were seduced by every ban,
> You charged like a bull through every red light,
> And no one could turn you from your path.
> But if all the paths are opened,
> Where do we go, and with whom?
> How would you find your way then?[21]

Another, and more fundamental development of the early 1980s was the rise of a new type of group and music called, predictably enough, New Wave. They sang almost exclusively about the daily life of young people like themselves, about what they enjoyed, such as drinking, making love, lying on the beach, obtaining new clothes or a walkman, and about the impediments to pleasure, such as parents, having to work, having no money and nowhere to go. The Leningrad group Kino, for example, did a whole series of songs about the life of a Soviet beatnik. 'No money and nowhere to go' are recurring themes in their songs. The lyrics and their messages are examined in more detail in the section on attitudes and lifestyles. Suffice it to say here that the growth in the movement began to cause a serious reconsideration on the part of officialdom.

In February 1981, the Leningrad City Council decreed into existence the Leningrad Rock Club, a move that paved the way for the strategy adopted nationwide since the spring of 1986. Undoubtedly the KGB, with an eye to public order and easier surveillance, had a say in this decision, but it was nevertheless something the rock movement had been seeking for years. Several attempts had been made by rock musicians and fans to open a rock club. Sometimes the proposals submitted to the city authorities were almost comical in view of the identity of their authors: 'The rock club sets itself the goal of attracting youth to a wide range of creative activities, of raising the cultural level of visual presentation and ideological artistic content in such performances, and likewise portraying and propagandising the best examples of national and international music in the given genre.'[22]

Kolya Mikhailov, the current President of the Rock Club, explains why the Rock Club was eventually created: 'It was the powerful initiative from below and the desire of officials somehow to control the concert activity of the bands.'[23] At the beginning of 1981 the number of concerts in the city had sharply decreased, since the groups had no permission to give official performances, while the city administration had become fairly effective at restraining the informal sessions. But there were over fifty known bands in Leningrad and a colossal, unfulfilled craving for concerts and socialising existed. Also, the official attitude to rock seemed to have softened. So, as Mikhailov says:

> The musicians and concert organisers bombarded the municipal organisations with requests to resolve the problem. And in the end we got a helping hand from the Centre for Individual Amateur Performance (CIAP) [an organisation co-ordinating all types of amateur artistic activity, music, theatre, film-making and dance ensembles on behalf of the trade unions]. At that time CIAP had just undergone a major change of personnel, including the appointment of a new chief, and almost all of them were women. They joked with us that if they lost their jobs because of us, at least their husbands could feed them.[24]

The authorities in Leningrad, under the Party leadership of the less than benevolent Grigory Romanov, were not renowned for their liberalism. With respect to youth they realised, however, that heavy-handedness was not the answer. The forced underground status of the rock movement put it beyond control. For the authorities a rock club would provide a convenient means of control as well as lessening the incidence of public disorder associated with the rock community. Victor Tsoi, leader of the group Kino, explained to me, 'It was better for them to have five hundred people going wild at a rock concert than have them fighting on the streets.'[25]

At first many bands were reluctant to join this new institution. It was given the 500-seat Theatre of Popular Creativity on Rubinstein Street as its home. It was also given a charter and an organisational structure that included a Council, an artistic committee and a censor. Only songs passed by the censor were allowed to be performed at concerts held at or under the auspices of the Rock Club. It was this stipulation that accounted for the initially small number of bands that applied for registration. As it turned out the process of censorship was not too severe:

> Lyrics must be approved before they can be performed at the Rock Club. This censorship is the responsibility of a woman who works as a full-time employee of the Club, a member of the Journalists' Union. That is her job and, most importantly, her responsibility. She is basically sympathetic and doesn't cut much, only what would bring many problems for her, the musicians and the Rock Club as a whole. She does what she feels has to be done otherwise we might transgress some limit and cause scandals and problems. The musicians themselves know this so they would never submit anything explicitly defiant.[26]

Since early 1987 censorship has been relaxed still further.

The Rock Club was supposed to arrange concerts in the city as well as at the Club, offer technical assistance, provide rehearsal space and assist in raising the standard of the groups. Starved of funds and wracked by internal squabbling between official representatives and those of the rock movement, it got off to a slow start. As the problems gradually resolved themselves more groups registered. The creative integrity of those bands already registered had not been seen to have been impeded. They included such 'supergroups' as Aquarium. Concerts were held more regularly, though still often subject to last-minute cancellation. Bands continued to record albums for the unofficial distribution system and to play concerts in towns without rock clubs, sometimes at the invitation of the local Komsomol. The Rock Club led to an improvement in the behaviour of the rock movement. Although many still remained convinced that it was little more than a convenient observatory for the KGB, the majority believed that their own concessions to officialdom were worthwhile given the increased level of rock activity. This rise from the underground also attracted a new audience that could become acquainted with domestic rock without the tension that underground status often caused. In 1983, however, those who had remained underground were given reason to believe that they had made the right decision.

The accession of Andropov following Brezhnev's death signalled a new era in all spheres of Soviet society. The leadership placed more emphasis on the need for discipline and ideological purity. Andropov's alleged affection for jazz did not extend to rock. Speaking at the July 1983 Plenum of the Party Central Committee of the Communist Party he said, 'It is intolerable to see the occasional emergence on a wave of popularity of musical bands with repertoires of a dubious nature.'[27] This speech signalled the start of an anti-rock campaign: 'All the powers of the state came into action. The ideologists produced the ideas, the Ministry of Culture issued the instructions and the local authorities and concert agencies got down to purging the rock scene.'[28] *Komsomolskaya pravda* was soon reporting: 'Much is being said about the unfavourable condition of the light musical genre, about the appearance of a series of programmes of doubtful worth. The responsible cultural authorities should launch a general review of [musical] collectives with the aim of taking the necessary actions to enhance their professionalism.'[29] This marked the start of what has been called the 'Soviet crusade against rock'.[30] In the main the crusade was against those rock groups and vocal/instrumental ensembles that the state had either created or coaxed up from the amateur movement.

Many actions were taken against these groups. The authorities put a stop to concerts and ordered a 'rehearsal' period in which the groups were supposed to produce repertoires consistent with the new ideological mood. In future, 80 per cent of the music in each concert had to be comprised of work by members of the Union of Composers. Members of this influential and conservative body were indignant at seeing their monopoly in songwriting broken by upstart young musicians, at seeing a decline in sales of their records as a result of the activity of these musically illiterate charlatans.[31]

The remaining songs had to go before the artistic committees of the responsible concert agencies. Evidently the groups had no choice but to abide by these rules. As *Sovetskaya kultura* put it, 'Many of the bands have made corrections to their repertoire, filling it with works by masters of Soviet music, decisively paying attention to patriotic songs or to political themes.'[32] The remaining groups (about forty in all) who failed to meet these stringent requirements were disbanded.

The campaign did not miss the amateur movement either, and several decrees and statutes were introduced in an attempt to gain control over it, or at least to ensure the situation did not deteriorate. In 1985, in the closing stages of the campaign, the Soviet Culture Ministry's Moscow Research Centre on the Arts released the following figures: 70 000 pop or rock groups existing in the Soviet Union; 145 of these, whose members were employees of the state concert agencies, were considered to be professional bands; 29 552 of the remainder were declared amateur bands registered with either the local authorities or trade union clubs. This left 40 000 rock and pop groups whose only contact with the state was with the local police and, occasionally, the KGB.[33]

Order No.67 issued by the USSR Ministry of Higher and Specialised Education on 22 August 1984, concerning 'Measures for the regulation of activities of vocal/instrumental groups in higher and intermediate specialised educational establishments, and for the improvement of the ideological/artistic standard of their repertoires' meant:

1. Reinforcement of control over the formation of amateur vocal/instrumental groups and their performances; a condition for forming a new vocal/instrumental group is to produce a certificate permitting the right to perform in public.
2. A ban on independent organisation of performances.
3. The compilation of repertoires and programmes high in ideological content.
4. Strict control over the broadcasting of 'musical variety programmes' where student construction gangs are working, and at rest centres, sports and health camps, student halls of residence, etc'.[34] This last measure was aimed at ensuring that *magnetizdat* tapes would not be played under official auspices. Other decrees in a similar vein were passed by regional trade union and Komsomol committees.

Initially these measures had a disastrous impact on the rock movement. For six months not a single concert took place in Moscow. In Leningrad, however, the Rock Club seemed to offer some protection against the worst effects of the campaign and its work continued largely unimpeded. Mindful of this, Artyem Troitsky, the Soviet Union's most liberal writer on rock and pop music, wrote an article in March 1984 in *Komsomolskaya pravda* that advocated an extension of the Rock Club experiment to other towns. He later commented,

I wrote that it was stupid to outlaw rock groups, that they would only go deeper underground. What was needed was to work with the musicians and 'cultivate' them. It was an extremely reasonable, harmless and liberal piece, written from an official point of view in which the Leningrad and Riga rock clubs were cited as positive examples. But even this brought forth a frenzied reaction from the culture bureaucracy – after all, the article had implied idleness and incompetence on their part in acting on the principle that it was easier to ban something than to act positively . . . Soon I discovered that I too had been banned. In every editorial office I visited I found sour expressions on colleagues' faces and heard the shattering words: 'The boss said working with you is not recommended.'[35]

By 1985 the worst of the campaign was over. In Leningrad the Rock Club had become an indispensable base for a much enlarged collection of rock bands. In other places the ban had created a sense of confinement and repression in which underground movements flourish. As the floodgates gradually opened, the long-concealed talent flooded the country and was fêted in the press. Moscow in particular spawned hundreds of New Wave groups.

The events of the very recent past and prospects for the future are examined in the last section of this chapter. The next section looks at the bands and audiences of the New Wave, and their lives and attitudes. It is this that the authorities are, for the first time, trying to understand rather than to ignore or repress.

THE LENINGRAD ROCK MUSIC COMMUNITY: STRATEGY FOR SURVIVAL

The Soviet rock community is not easy to define. It encompasses people of different backgrounds and ages. On the one hand, it is a relatively small band of musicians, avant-garde artists, writers and other 'cultural workers'. Some participants see similarities between their community and the artistic avant-garde of the 1920s. As an avant-garde, it influences youth fashion and ideology in the same way that pop and rock heroes do in the West. However, the conditions in which it grew have made the movement much less elitist than its Western counterpart. The groups of the New Wave emerged from the same background as their audience, they articulate the values of their audience rather than formulating them, which results in reinforcing the attitudes expressed. In one *samizdat* manuscript on rock, the late Vladimir Vysotsky is described as 'the first Soviet rocker'.

Vysotksy's constituency was far broader than is that of the rock movement, but there is a similarity in that the affection and respect afforded both to today's rockers and to Vysotsky derive from the lyricists' intimate knowledge of each listener's life.

Leningrad, for historical reasons, has been close to the West metaphorically as well as physically. This is one of the reasons why rock has become so well established there and why Leningrad has had considerable influence over the rock community as a whole. Furthermore, outside the Baltic Republics (Latvia, Lithuania and Estonia), the rock community is largely confined to large cities in the Russian Republic, such as Moscow, Novosibirsk, Sverdlovsk and Gorky, or to cities with large Russian populations, such as Kiev. Life in these metropolises tends to be similar enough to evince similar responses from their young people. All the same, Leningrad must be recognised as a somewhat extreme example.

One of the most striking features of the rock community is the distinction it makes between itself and what it sees as 'official society'. Although most members of the rock community have a genuine affection for their fellow countrymen and women, they scorn the acceptance of 'Soviet' values by the majority. For example, patriotism, instilled by the state through all the agencies of education and propaganda, is by now a heart-felt emotion for most Soviet citizens (especially for those who survived the Second World War). For the rock community, too, patriotism and love for the motherland is still a relevant value. But within Russia this is expressed predominantly outside the context of the Soviet system, relating only to 'Mother Russia'. For example, the Leningrad rock community, acutely aware and proud of its cultural and historical heritage, often refers to the city in conversation, in lyrics and in *samizdat* as Petersburg, or simply Peter. Though it does not have quite the same emotional significance as the dropping of 'London' from Londonderry by Republicans of that city in Northern Ireland, this rejection of the name of Lenin is nevertheless symbolic of the rock community's desire to disassociate itself from the Soviet system.

One radical difference between the rock community and its Western counterpart of the late 1960s and early 1970s is that it does not seek to change the system. Freedom is perceived as a spiritual phenomenon that can be achieved by living, as far as possible, beyond the realm of official life. Boris Grebenshchikov explains that 'as long as the people in charge do not know how to react to the spiritual feeling, they are missing the whole point. They cannot control what they do not believe exists.'[36] Another musician, Mikhail Barazikhin, suggests how to achieve freedom from the Soviet state in one of the most popular and radical songs of recent times:

They monitor us from birth,	I say to you: Get out of control,
Our kind uncles and aunts,	Tear down these walls,
We grow up an obedient breed,	Sing what you want, not what
We sing what they want,	you're told
We live how they want.	Get out of control, we can be
Looking out at the terrorists	free.[37]
above,	

This process of disassociation from official culture often begins in the late teens. As in all industrialised countries, this is the age when young people leave the institutionalised setting that school provides and are forced to make decisions about their future, requiring an examination of their past. For many in the rock community this process leads to the conclusion that much of the past has been a waste of time. The formality, universality and rigidity of the education system leave many with a sour taste; state-glorified ethics and heroes become targets of irreverent wit and sarcasm. The exploits of Yury Gagarin and the Soviet space programme are recurring themes for jokes and satirical songs. The leading icon of Soviet ideology, Lenin, suffers a similar fate. Anyone aware of the general high affection held for Lenin by the population at large, regardless of the crimes of his successors, will recognise the significance of this. Nothing Soviet is holy for the rock movement.

Many rock fans go on to higher education. For many of these students a motivation to learn soon gives way to the realisation that a student lifestyle can offer the leisure time essential for full participation in the rock community. Poor attendance and dropping out are not infrequent, and fear of failure becomes less important as they realise that success is a guarantee of privilege only in a system from which they are moving away. The rock comunity as a whole gives the appearance of having a high level of education, at least by Western standards. Reading is one of the universal pastimes of many Soviet people and it is not rejected by the rock community. The works of Western authors are especially popular. Furthermore, the rock community has access to many *samizdat* publications of unpublished Soviet and Western authors, often in translation. Although many of these young people are auto-didactics, some credit must go to the official education system that provided them with a platform from which to start answering questions that the system itself never raised.

Work is another area of concern and one of much relevance to the rock movement. The emphasis put upon work and its glorification in Soviet ideology is paid only lip-service by the population as a whole. In the case of the rock community, work is at best seen as a necessary evil to be done first to keep within the law and second to earn a living. The key determinants in job selection are not wages, but hours and ease of work. Thus, a job involving two 24-hour shifts per week stoking the furnaces of central-heating systems for 80 rubles a month (the average industrial wage is approximately 200 rubles per month) is a desirable occupation. Such part-time jobs that comply with the labour laws are relatively rare. Rather than take on more onerous tasks, a sizeable minority of the rock community, including many of the musicians, do no work at all and thus put themselves outside the law. They are prepared to risk this 'parasitical' status rather than sacrifice their time to a state to which they feel little allegiance. Further, the low wages that are paid for the sort of work they seek gives little incentive to work.

For many others it is not possible to find work. In Moscow and Leningrad there are thousands of young people living without official residential permission (*propiska*) for these cities. They have come from small towns to be near to the 'centre of action'. Without this *propiska* they cannot gain employment. This situation often leads to a precarious existence. Money can only be made on the black market and there is a constant fear that even the briefest police check may result in a prison sentence. Rock fans often travel regularly between Moscow and Leningrad, but undocumented people (i.e. persons without residential permits and work cards) do so even more often. The possession of a recent train ticket from a different city can be enough to deter questioning by the police.

Work is very much a secondary activity for the rock community. Although many hold full-time jobs, this does not rank highly in their general consciousness. Work is seen as an impediment to the pursuance of pleasure and is cast out of mind, out of hours. These attitudes and practices of the rock movement with regard to work are one of the main causes of the antipathy felt towards it by the general public. Few people enjoy work, yet the necessity of being seen to work is as firmly embedded in the general Soviet consciousness as it is in the Soviet criminal code.

Parasitism, illegal residence, speculation and drug use, though not in the mainstream of the life of the rock community, are very much associated with this outlook. This brings the state into the affairs of the rock movement through the police and KGB. The poor and uneasy relations go back many years. Before the establishment of the Leningrad Rock Club in 1981, police and the KGB often took action against the rock movement. Just carrying a guitar and having long hair were once ample reason for interrogation, and leaders of the rock movement were often detained by the KGB. Concerts were raided and broken up and sound equipment and instruments confiscated. Today the police in Leningrad also intervene in concerts to ensure that 'wild outbreaks of bourgeois decadence', like dancing in the aisles, do not occur. Incidents in which musicians are arrested at concerts are still frequent, leading to potentially violent confrontation in the atmosphere of a rock concert. Take, for example, the opening night of the Leningrad Rock Club's annual season in 1986. As an American music journal reported,

> Aquarium is greeted with a standing ovation. Boris Grebenshchikov is not smiling. 'Aquarium is not going to play tonight', he says, 'and we want you to know why. People in this hall are breaking the law. They are overstepping their authority.' He briefly states that out in the lobby, men have been detaining and questioning many people, including musicians. Andrei Otryaskin, one of the most talented musicians in the country, had his head slammed against a wall when he tried to resist. 'Tonight was supposed to be a celebration,' says Grebenshchikov, 'but as long as these things are happening, this is not our Rock Club and there is no reason for celebration.' The crowd begins to buzz with anger. With the house lights up, the buzz turns into a roar, and the roar rises to a crescendo. Soon rhythmic stamping rocks the building. Ten minutes later, with the noise in the theatre still building – and rapidly taking on the mood of violence – Aquarium returns to the stage. Grebenshchikov delivers the verdict, 'We will play for you, and only to you. We play for those who have come to hear music.' The musicians quickly fall into the reggae lope of 'Living in Babylon', and Grebenshchikov sings: 'We're living in Babylon/This city is Bablyon/But we can own our own minds.' The song erupts into a full-blown roar as 400 people stand on chairs and in the aisles. Every Leningrad musician in the theatre soon makes his way to the stage to stand with Aquarium ... and the Leningrad Rock Club vibrates with the defiant sound of rock and roll.[38]

Although there is no longer so much intervention in concerts as there used to be, big events are usually well-attended by uniformed police and plain-clothed KGB officers. Such intrusion into the 'holy temples' of the rock movement sours the movement's attitude to the police. Besides this, many have real reason to fear an investigation of their personal circumstances. The fact that so much repression was used in the early days of the rock community has left a legacy of bitterness that will take a long time to erode. Nowadays police attention is concentrated on much tougher opponents than hippies and rockers – such as the soccor fans, the notorious *Lyubery* and the *Afgantsy*.[39]

It is not only with regard to work that some of the rock community break their obligation to the state. Army service is an ordeal to be avoided at all costs. Higher education at a university or parental influence can sometimes ensure a shorter conscription or service with officer rank. The ony other way to avoid military service is by physical or mental sickness. Drastic measures are sometimes taken to meet these criteria, the most common being to slash one's own wrists at a non-critical point. The resultant month in a mental institution and life-long scar are considered well worth it in order to avoid the discipline, boredom and frugality of conscript life. The large hippy movement is every bit as pacifist as Western hippies and hippies try to avoid military service. The war in Afghanistan has increased pacifism in the community as a whole; there are many anti-war songs in circulation, some written in Afghanistan itself.

The rock movement is generally not overtly political. The Soviet system is thought of cynically, and government and Party policy is met with distrust. Awareness of this may be a crucial factor behind the policies of the new leadership towards youth. The strategy of disassociation means that the topic of politics, both internal and external, is rarely brought up; the lyrics of songs have tended to focus more on the lives and 'spiritual baggage' necessary for this disassociated status. Overtly political songs are becoming more common now, perhaps a reflection of the fact that the rock movement *can* make a difference in this new era. During the Brezhnev years, life underground, though political in nature, did not give rise to a coherent opposition philosophy. The sheer impossibility of achieving anything by legitimate means made apathy the dominant philosophy of the rock movement. Songs directly concerned with the political system contained no suggestion of positive action. This did not make them less acute in their political message. The Moscow group DK are especially adept at pointing out the truth behind the idyll of the 1970s and early 1980s, as the following lyrics illustrate:

I'm a closed citizen, lads and
 lasses,
I've a closed family.
Now I'm going to the closed shop
To buy some closed wine.
At home I'll crack it open
With my closed wife
And polish off my closed booze.
I'll hit the sack feeling queer.
After I've opened the closed
 window
At the entrance door an
 armoured car
will flash in the moonlight.
Tomorrow I'll give my speech
Which I've never set eyes on
 before.
The bloke who wrote it won't
 find out
So we can laugh ourselves silly.
So long as no one interrupts me.
I'll try a serious face in the
 mirror,
And go to the exemplary
 workers.
I'll test dung with my finger.
I'll wrinkle my brow for the
 photographers.
I can tell you, just imagine the
 fun,

I go down to the people, smile,
 and say,
My hopes and your hopes are the
 same,
You work, and as for me, I am
 working too.
Watch out traffic police, here I
 come.
There's a bird waiting for me
In a closed car. My Beloved
 Mary.
And after that, say no more.
The driver will wait for us for a
 while.
And then home again to the
 family to meet their dad.
Then to the closed doctor,
And put on a little show for him.
Then I'll fly down the avenue
And with the stylish flashing light
I'll frighten the ravens and
 crows.
I know all the questions in
 advance.
What I am is no secret.
I am a man of the people,
 the people chose me
And raised me over the years.
That's how it is, boom, boom,
 fuck you,
That's how it is.[40]

A good knowledge of the West, coming from contact with foreign tourists and students, Western radio stations and available Soviet sources, allows the rock community to make comparison; and it gives them a reference point from which to judge their own system. The economic wellbeing of the West leads many to assume that the market system, based on open pluralist democracy, is the only viable system of government and economy. Knowledge of unemployment, poverty, no free health service (in America) does not deter them from this belief, although such phenomena meet with sympathy. Given the lack of variety in their own lives, members of the rock community tend to look at the West in a largely uncritical fashion. Very few of them make the distinction between socialism as a philosophy and socialism in the USSR. Thus, the Gorbachov message of a new socialist approach has so far provoked little enthusiasm.

The 'red press' (*krasny* press) is another institution generally shunned by the rock community. Though foreign journals of specific interest and magazines about life abroad, such as *Angliya* in the case of Britain, are widely read, Soviet periodicals such as *Pravda* and the central youth press are ignored. The Moscow group, *Zvuki Mu*, has a song about *Soyuzpechat* (the state newspaper distribution system):

On the mornings when I
Finally go home,
Is when I want what I can
Never get.
It was the fresh printed
Papers
That taught me to dream.
It was *Soyuzpechat*
That taught us how to wait.

When you pass me by
Don't make that kind of face
As if you couldn't give a damn
What the papers and this
Country say about us.
And remember, the money
We all make is false money.
Counterfeit paper –
Soyuzpechat.[41]

Such sentiments apply equally to the electronic media. The diet of Soviet achievements and war films that was earlier the main fare of Soviet TV led the Leningrad group *Televizor* to write the song 'Your Television is talking to you':

Two hundred and twenty cold
 volts.
The system is reliable, won't
 break down,
And the evening will give you
 nothing.
Programmes are always the
 same.
People are eating, they feel
 good,

It's the age of electronic
 enjoyment.
Someone here needs an electric
 shock,
Then I'll feel an awakening.
Leave me alone, I'm alive!
I want to think with my own
 mind
I don't want to name heroes,
I don't want to talk of blood.[42]

What emerges is a community whose strategy for survival in an erstwhile hostile and unappealing environment has been to disassociate

itself from maintsteam culture. Boris Grebenshchikov thinks that
this 'New Wave' movement 'is not pro-Soviet because it knows
nothing about the Soviet way of thinking. It is not anti-Soviet; it deals
with quite another reality of people who don't think of themselves as
citizens of such-and-such state or system, but deal with each other as
real people without connecting it to ideology.'[43]

Pedro Ramet says of 'counterculture' in communist regimes that,
broadly defined,

> any culture which challenges the Party's official culture which is
> premised on the concept of a single legitimate, general interest, can
> be seen as a counterculture. More narrowly defined, counter-
> culture could be seen as a set of ideas, orientations, tastes and
> assumptions which differ systematically from those of the dominant
> culture, recognising that dominant culture is not the same as
> official culture.[44]

By both these definitions the rock community can be considered a
counterculture. For confirmation of this, and to draw some comparisons with Western youth counterculture, it is useful to look more
closely at the lifestyles of the rock community.

SEX, DRUGS AND ROCK'N'ROLL

On Radio Moscow's North American service, Joe Adamov, the
veteran presenter of the Moscow postbag, recently answered a
Canadian enquiry about whether Soviet young people were ever
bored. In keeping with the spirit of *glasnost* Adamov admitted the
existence of this phenomenon and made no secret of the fact that this
was due to the lack of sports and other public facilities.[45] This is
indicative of what the offical attitude towards youth has been. It is the
responsibility of the state to provide entertainment for youth, not for
youth to provide its own. The state monopoly of all buildings and
recreational facilities leads it to believe that boredom can be eliminated by expenditure on such. Given the rock community's rejection
of state institutions, this means that, apart from concerts and a few
cafes, the rock community spends much of its leisure time either in
private flats or outside on the streets. The Rock Club is one of the few
institutions set up by the state in which the rock community feels it
can be its own boss. The general lack of somewhere to go is a
constant theme of New Wave rock lyrics.

Guys and gals are walking the
streets
Hoping for goodness knows
what.
Guys and gals are sitting on
benches
In entrances and cinemas.
Their personal life depends
On problems of housing.
And if there weren't such
problems
Everyone would have a harem,
oh yes.
At home there's mother and
father,
No room at hotels.
The porter stands guard at the
student residence
As unyielding as Mohammed
himself.

Kissing at the entrance is so
uncomfortable, in
the streets
You get frozen all over.
People are passing by,
There is no peace of mind.
In summer we can go together to
the woods,
But it takes an hour to get there.
And if the local yobs get you,
You risk being beaten into a pile
of shit.
And so boys and girls are
walking on,
Especially in winter.
There's nowhere for them to
make love.[46]

Leningrad has one public building in which the rock community
has become almost sitting tenants: Restaurant Moskva, universally
know as Cafe Saigon. The name 'Saigon' dates back to the 1960s
when the originators of the rock movement first became interested in
Western youth counter-culture and it has long been a hang-out for
young people. 'It's a magical place, a place of power,' Aquarium
cellist Seva Gakkel says of the Cafe, located on the main thorough-
fare, Nevsky Prospect. 'All the crossroads of the city go through it.
When you're waiting for something to happen but don't know what it
is, the best place to go is Saigon. And before the Rock Club, when
there was no advertising for underground concerts you could find the
information there.'[47] More than a meeting point Saigon is a monument to the way in which the rock movement instils a sense of
community. The cafe is the first stop for visitors arriving in town for
the first time. Though generally the movement consists of groups of
friends, *tusovki* in local parlance, these groups have many tangents
leading out to numerous places. Although from a wide variety of
personal backgrounds, they are united by a common language, rock
music, which is an expression of the desire for independence, first of
mind, then of body. Kostya Kinchev, leader of the Leningrad group

Alisa (Alice), sings a song that unfailingly provokes rapport with the audience:

> The beginning impulse, the ball is in play,
> A search for contact, the searching of hands,
> I've begun to sing in my own language,
> I'm sure it was not something sudden,
> And I write verses for those who
> Don't wait for answers to today's question.
> I sing for those who go their own way.
> I'm glad if someone has understood me . . .
> We're together, we're together![48]

Rock lyrics are not the only common language of the rock community, it has a jargon of its own. Many of the words originated from the hippy movement which has since been assimilated into the rock community, though maintaining distinct ideals and customs. Evidence of the responsibility of the West for the movement's origins can be discerned in this jargon, *Parents, police, shoes, hair, price, flat* and *high-life* are all now 'Russian' words. Others are semi-Russified; *statsi* (States) for Americans, or *vpisatsya na nait* for 'to find somewhere to stay the night'.

This Western influence is omnipresent in the rock movement. Western clothes continue to fetch a premium price on the black market and at rock concerts it is sometimes hard to remember, judging by clothes, hair styles and other ornamentation (walkman, digital watch) that you are in the USSR. It is Western music that is most sought after by the rock community and members are generally extremely knowlegeable about it. The rock *samizdat* publications, such as *Roxy* (Leningrad), *Smochok* (Moscow) and *Blin* (Novosibirsk) are full of information about the latest Western releases and rock gossip. Articles from the Western musical press and interviews with Western musicians, translated into Russian, are common. Not surprisingly, much of the music played by Soviet rock groups is Western in style, but this does not necessarily mean, as some contend, that the existence of rock in Eastern Europe and the Soviet Union is evidence of the power of Western cultural imperialism.

Rock is a Western genre, as was ballet and opera. The lyrics have always been more significant than the music for Soviet youth, and their themes relate to the concerns of their Soviet audience. The Leningrad writer Alexander Zhitinsky explains what was wrong with the official condemnation of the rock movement as a product of the West. Writing in *Teatr* he says,

> Others [opponents of rock] have tried to talk about Western influence, but to do so by then [the early 1980s] was simply foolish. The number of spontaneously arising groups was calculated to already be in the thousands. Getting no moral or material support, young people in Leningrad, Sverdlovsk, etc., acquired guitars and composed songs. Evidently this expressed a vital need. They clearly wanted to say something. But they spoke their own language, inaccessible to 'adults'. The words were undoubtedly Russian, but the notions, ideas, feelings ... All this music has social concerns different from those in the West. These have only recently been revealed, although they were evident for a long time.[49]

Fetishism for Western commodities is more a protest against the Soviet retail distribution system and its lack of variety than an affirmation of solidarity with the West, although obviously fashion, in the long term, affects attitudes. Excessive concentration on fashion has provoked some songwriters to point out how ludicrous it can become:

The Ancient Greeks wore togas
And never had any cares.
I've been sitting home all week
Until mum finds a pair of jeans.
It's not a whim or principle.
Mum, if you don't buy them,
I'll tell you straight,
Tomorrow I'll run away from
home,

Mum, mum, I'll run, I'll run, I'll
run away . . . ,
The Romans used to wear tunics,
And I've lost sleep over jeans.
The wicked West dreamed up
this fashion,
That's why we have to pay such a
dreadful price.[50]

Having created for itself a mass of leisure time at the expense of work, the rock community has the problem of filling this time in a situation of almost nowhere to go and no money to spend. Apart from the brief Leningrad summer, this means that the rock community finds itself, for climatic reasons, largely confined to apartments. For those with flats in the city centre this means a busy lifestyle. In common with youth across the industrialised world, Leningrad youth when at a loose end tends to congregate in the city centre. Despite . the inferiority of housing in the older buildings which predominate in the city centre, a flat here is a prized possession in the rock community. Drinking tea, talking, joking, smoking, listening to music, such is the range of activities available within the confines of four walls, as any long-term unemployed young person in the West will testify. What the British New Wave group, The Stranglers, termed 'hanging around' is a common condition of the rock community, be it on the beach in summer, the parks in autumn or the bed-sitting room in winter. The boredom and apathy this may lead to among some young people in the West have caused the Soviet rock movement to adopt a similar strategy in overcoming them – excessive consumption of alcohol and growing usage of drugs.

Although Western modern youth counter-culture has always involved use of drugs, its Soviet counterpart differs in three respects. First, the most common medium of escape is vodka, not marijuana. Second, excessive consumption of alcohol is a universal feature of mainstream Soviet culture. Third, as a consequence of the second, abstainers are much less frequent than in the West. It would be unfair to portray the rock community as a society for aspiring alcoholics, but vodka does play a central role in the lives of the rock community, especially amongst musicians. Artyem Troitsky has suggested that the psychodelia of the Western rock movement has its counterpart in Soviet alcoholism. Certainly drinking is the activity most commonly referred to in Soviet rock lyrics:

I came home,
As usual alone again,
My house is empty.
The telephone suddenly rings,
They will knock on the door
And shout from the street
That I've slept enough,
And a drunken voice will say:
'Give us some food.'
My friends always go through life
At a march,
Waiting only at
Beer kiosks.
My house is empty;
Now it's full of people

For the thousandth time,
My friends are drinking wine
  there.
Someone's been in the toilet a
  long time
And broken the window.
To tell the truth, I couldn't give a
  damn,
I laugh,
Though it's not always funny.
I get very angry
When they say to live
Like I do now is impossible.
After all, I live,
And no one can deny that.[51]

The anti-alcohol campaign, launched in 1985, has had little effect on the Leningrad rock community. Whereas many provincial towns are virtually 'dry' zones, alcohol supply to Moscow and Leningrad continues. The substantial price increases on vodka have done more to change consumer preference than to make people sober. Shops that specialise in vodka sales are almost devoid of queues, whereas a queue for cheap, strong, fortified wine can take all afternoon. The rigidity of opening hours, from two until seven p.m., has made the community much more conscious of the time of day. Others in the rock community seek a different form of oblivion.

Marijuana usage is long established in the USSR, but the amount of hard drugs being taken is on the increase. There are said to be 48 000 registered drug addicts in the Soviet Union, mainly users of heroin and opium brought from the Central Asian Republics and from bordering countries, and also a large amount of medicinal drugs diverted from their intended use in the health service. In an effort to stop these diversions, which occur en route from farm to factory to hospital, the Soviet government recently announced that it is ceasing the farming of opium poppies and wild hemp and will import all necessary opiates. Until recently, registering addiction guaranteed treatment similar to that given to a convict, which certainly restricted the number who would otherwise seek it. As in the West, drug users have their own culture and language: *dvigatsya* – to fix; *mashina* – a syringe; *pykhat* – to smoke a joint; *travka* (from the Russian for grass) or *plan* – marijuana. Much of the cannabis used comes from the North Caucasus and some comes from Afghanistan. Ex-servicemen from Afghanistan have played a big part in increasing the scope and nature of drug use. In recent years enforcement of the drug laws has become tougher, as have judicial penalties. Possession of even a small amount of cannabis, once merely a cautionable offence, can now carry a sentence of five years' hard labour.

Despite this it seems that drug use is increasing, finding a broader spectrum of users than before, and that this growth is leading to the rise of a drug industry. Such a situation must seriously worry the Soviet authorities who are aware of the extent of the problem in the West. The growth in drug taking and extensive alcohol abuse must be a major determinant in new measures taken to promote dialogue with youth. As an expression of boredom, alienation and estrangement, alcohol and drug abuse surely have no equal.

Some aspects of the behaviour of the rock movement reflect that of society at large. One is the status of women in the movement. There are very few female singers, musicians or artists in what might be considered the elite of the movement. Although women are numerous in the community as a whole, they play a secondary role. The making of tea, cooking of food and suchlike are services expected by the men and delivered by the women. This is an incongruous detail in the general picture of similarity to Western youth behaviour. Moreover, the treatment of women as 'sex' objects is rife in exclusively male conversation. The response of women within the rock community to such treatment nevertheless differs markedly from that of women in society at large.

If the Soviet Union has a reputation for prudishness, then the rock community must be seen as licentious in the extreme.[52] the practicalities of Soviet housing and the lifestyles of the rock community (often staying with friends) means a lack of secrecy in sex that privacy affords. This weakens the taboos about sex. Men, as in maintream Russian culture, are rarely faithful to their wives or girlfriends. What is surprising is the number of women who take the same attitude. The aura of mystique about sex, still widespread among youth in many Western countries, is rare in the Leningrad rock community. In this they resemble American youth. This weakening of previously held values was, in America, one result of widespread access to the pill. Soviet poeple still lack a pharmaceutical solution to birth control, and the risky surgery of abortion remains widely used; often performed under local anaesthetic, it is an experience genuinely loathed and feared. Even so, some women have several abortions.

AIDS (*SPID* in the Russian acronym) was, until recently, seen as a distant Western disease, the butt of much humour and speculation. The Soviet media are now giving much more detailed information on the disease and testing centres have been opened in Moscow and Leningrad. In addition legislation has been enacted, including the compulsory testing of foreign residents. The Soviet rock community, with its many contacts with Westerners, relatively high proportion of drug users and homosexuals, is particularly vulnerable. Whether this will cause a change in sexual patterns like those said already to have occurred in the West is uncertain. An improvement in the quantity and quality of domestic contraceptives seems unlikely in the near future, and much of the Soviet rock community has a 'live hard, die young' attitude towards all its vices.

Despite occasionally seeming hell-bent on self-destruction, the rock community is on the whole relatively happy. Friendships are very close within the community and provide emotional and often financial support for companions. Humour, an essential ingredient for survival in any society, is ever present despite the often depressing reality that confronts young people. The rock community is generally intelligent and articulate and directs these attributes towards creative endeavour rather than political activism. The creation of music and art is not confined to the elite of the movement; the audience is just as active as its leaders, and the leaders are selected from the followers by the followers.

The major restriction upon the rock community is that its members cannot travel abroad. Being so knowledgeable and inquisitive about the West, the rock community feels this restriction particularly acutely. The many contacts its members have with Westerners and the ease with which Westerners can travel reinforce the feeling of isolation within their own society. The days when so many wanted to live in the West are over; the creation of an alternative society at home makes home more bearable. All the same, the desire to travel is in no way diminished. Nothing short of the lifting of this ban will ever fully reconcile the rock community to the Soviet state. In the meantime, the restructuring which the Soviet Union is now undergoing seems to have as one of its goals precisely such a reconciliation with youth.

PERESTROIKA: BUILDING BRIDGES AT HOME

Mikhail Gorbachov, addressing the January 1987 CPSU Central Committee Plenum, called for greater trust in young people.[53] Since then this attitude has been displayed by a number of officials in relation to the rock community. An editorial in *Roxy* recognised the depth of change:

> Yes, dear readers, it seems as if the kindergarten period has come to an end; judge for yourselves, rock clubs have opened in Novosibirsk, Odessa, Kharkov, Riga, Kiev, Sverdlovsk and elsewhere ... Aquarium has given ten concerts at the Olympic Sports Complex, right after UB40 played there. Discussions are taking place on releasing a compilation album of the Rock Club. There is still a long way to go, yet this situation puts a heavy responsibility upon us all.[54]

The attitude of the state towards the young has in the past often been based on falsehoods: 'We have lied loudly and brazenly, shut our eyes to the truth and compromised our principles. Enough! The time for chanting ritual hosannas is past. Our time has come, comrades.'[55] Official treatment of the rock community has been based largely on the same principles during the fifteen years of its existence in the Soviet Union. This treatment was assessed by a commentator in *Literaturnaya gazeta* as follows:

> Oh, if it were only possible to collect everything published about amateur rock. How few compassionate, warm words! How much evidence of ill will and 'playing safe' by editors. We distorted lyrics to prove how evil they were, we arbitrarily switched composers' names (imagine the fuss if we had done that with any of our recognised composers). We labelled Andrei Makarevich an apologist for primitivism, and many groups of singing Russian songs with an English accent. Who exactly do you mean? No one will suggest a name, neither readers nor musicians. Nobody's going to create trouble about a deliberate or mistaken slander; so you're not surprised to read in a serious article that there can be no such thing as Russian rock on account of the specific rhythmical structure of the Russian language. It turns out that rock is derivative, an artificial thorn in our culture. From this the conclusion follows: get out the garden shears, cut off the thorn and solve your problem.[56]

This article marked a watershed for the rock community. From then on comment and policies towards rock have become a barometer for testing the strength of opposition and support for *perestroika* by the various factions of the bureaucracy. This is a reflection of the difficulty the media and other agencies are having at a time when clear-cut instruction from the leadership is being replaced by ideological guidelines.

> When we are talking of the changes and consistency or inconsistency in the official Soviet attitude towards rock, we should bear in mind that Soviet society, the Soviet state, is now not at all as unanimous or solid as it used to be. Rock has become one of the strongest points of argument between the proponents and opponents of *perestroika*. Everybody says they are for *perestroika*, yet it is evident that everybody or every group in society understands *perestroika* in a very different way. Government at the top is no longer quick or ready to give its views about this or that subject, especially when it comes to a minor one like rock.[57]

Official attitudes as expressed by the media and concert and recording agencies, local Party and Komsomol officials, have taken a 'quantum leap'. Rock is undergoing a public analysis that Western rock only had from a small circle of sociologists and musicologists. Such serious treatment of an art form is fairly typical in the Soviet Union and is a sure sign that rock has achieved something approaching true recognition by the state. Before we look at what the consequences of this acceptance have been and what they might mean for the future, let us look at some of the changes that have taken place.

As mentioned earlier, it is the model of the Leningrad Rock Club that has been taken up by most authorities in towns where the rock community flourishes. In Moscow, a Rock Laboratory was set up under the auspices of the local Komsomol. This is significant in-asmuch as if the state wishes the rock community to join it in partnership it is the Komsomol that is the most logical agency for achieving this. The Rock Laboratory in Mocow has been very active, giving a platform for the many radical bands which had no outlet for their creative talents. Furthermore, censorship at the Laboratory is virtually non-existent. In Leningrad, after a few false starts, censor-ship has also been dropped. This weakening or removal of censorship is occurring at the same time that the lyrics are becoming more manifestly political. It may not yet have filtered down to the audience, but musicians are today the subject of much critical acclaim and analysis in the media and are being offered options never before available; they are inevitably being politicised by these changes that affect them directly.

One of the most striking examples of the new policies has been the promotion of Aquarium to near official status. One of the group's previously 'underground' albums has been released by *Melodiya* (selling 200 000 copies in a matter of hours). The sleeve notes, waxing lyrical about the genius of Soviet rock, were written by no less a figure than the renowned poet Andrei Voznesensky. Again the move to adopt Aquarium as the 'flagship of *glasnost*' is a replication of an old policy. The people who invited Time Machine and their leader Andrei Makarevich to leave the amateur or underground movement for the 'sanitised' and regulated world of professionalism are no longer in charge. All the same, many people suspect that Aquarium, too, will 'sell out' to the authorities. The group's leader Grebenshchi-kov, recently discussed these points in an interview with the *New York Times*. He said that they were so official now, so taken to heart, that the people who were with them before were not sure of them any more. Nobody could believe the system had changed. They thought

Aquarium must have changed. Later on he explicitly referred (in a personal communication to this author) to the comparisons drawn between him and Makarevich: 'Somewhere he switched to not exactly writing painful songs. From year to year, he became more and more polite, and now he is so polite nobody wants to listen to him. I'm mortally afraid of being like him. It's the biggest terror of my life.'

The Leningrad rock critic Alex Kan believes that there is nothing sinister about this promotion of Aquarium:

> Boris Grebenshchikov of 1986 or 1987 is not at all the Boris Grebenshchikov of seven or eight years ago. He changed and changed naturally. That was the natural evolution of an artist. He is not as aggressive, sarcastic or satirical as he was. He is much more mellow, both in music and in lyrics. This process coincided with the general evolution of society and [the emergence of] *perestroika*. And so it brought together the culture of the establishment and Aquarium. At a certain point they fitted each other very well and therefore Aquarium was exactly the band chosen as a banner of *perestroika* and rock.[58]

Other groups who would previously have laughed in the face of official invitations have also grasped the nettle, but many are more circumspect. Victor Tsoi, leader of Kino, explains that nowadays it is not enough to refuse to participate: 'Every week Leningrad Radio plays my songs. I ring them up and ask them not to, but they carry on. Until I'm allowed to play exactly what I want, I don't want this. I don't want people to think the world has really changed that much until it has.'[59] The Leningrad group Televizor expresses such sentiments in their song:

> Ok, so they let us break-dance,
> OK, so we can be happy sometimes.
> But still standing behind the column
> Is the man in the thin tie
> With cement in his eyes.[60]

Muzykalnaya zhizn has offered an alternative explanation: 'The majority of the rock groups do not want to be professional, even though the offer is made frequently.'[61]

Concerts are now held on a much more regular basis and at larger venues. The list of songs played by a group no longer has to be approved and although the police presence at concerts is at the same level, their intervention is less. I remember attending a concert in early 1986 at which the camera of a foreigner was confiscated by the KGB. In July 1987 at a *Zvuki Mu* concert a policeman actually cleared a place for my American friend carrying an expensive video camera. His other duty was to protect the video equipment of Leningrad Television which was also filming the concert. Central Television now broadcasts in the programme 'Musical Ring', an hour of Soviet and Western rock groups, every week. Many of the former are amateur groups.

Above all it has been *glasnost* that has brought the most significant changes to the rock community. The volte-face in attitude has been more striking in relation to the rock community than to any other facet of cultural life. The new policy and personnel changes in the Film Makers Union, for example, have certainly had wide-ranging effects on the industry, but cinematography did not have the added complication of having to be accepted as a valid artistic phenomenon. When a film was deemed inappropriate for public showing it was usually shelved in a dusty cupboard, the maker forgotten. The producers in the rock community, however, had been dragged out on to the pages of newspapers and presented, at worst, as criminals whose leaders were 'front men' for Western ideological subversion, and, at best, as misguided but correctable youth.

The extent of this U-turn has resulted in the press having to eat a lot of humble pie. So has the Party and Komsomol. Young people have shown themselves to be in no mood for compromise and the range and scope of their activities have finally persuaded the powers-that-be that it is possible to compromise, to give youth the independence it strives for without it challenging the legitimacy of the state. One significant step the leadership has taken in this respect is to stop pinning all hopes on the Komsomol. The emergence of thousands of unoffical youth associations had made the authorities realise that they have no alternative but to accept the degree of independence that young people have already created for themselves. Gradually permission is being granted for the formation of officially independent forms of youth association. *Moscow News* has reported on a first step taken in this direction – the Statute on Amateur Associations and Hobby Clubs adopted on 13 May 1986:

> The Statute stipulates that a group of people united by common interests can form an association under the aegis of a sponsor whom they can choose themselves – for example, a housing administration, trade union committee, a sport or cultural agency,

while remaining autonomous. The association can exist at the expense of the sponsoring agency, on membership dues or on a self-repayment basis.[62]

This is hardly the complete freedom of association guaranteed by the Soviet Constitution, but it is a step in the right direction.

The Communist Party has only itself to blame for the attitude of today's youth and the onus is on the Party to prove that *perestroika* is a real, enduring and meaningful process. The Party and its agencies know that if they are to recapture the trust and leadership of youth, they have to do so not only by policies, but by example. They should heed the words of Zvuki Mu:

> They used to say we had to
>   strike proudly forward.
> Now they say we have to
>   jump proudly forward.
> But we have to turn round
>   first,
> And they never taught us to turn round.[63]

CONCLUSIONS

1. In this era of *glasnost* it is becoming easier to study such phenomena as youth deviance. However, we should not be misled into thinking that these phenomena are new. The history of the rock music community demonstrates the length of time, nearly two decades, in which such phenomena have existed. This duration coincides roughly with the Brezhnev years. This is no accident. These years witnessed stagnation in all spheres of social and economic life and led to a growth of youth awareness and counter-culture.

Those who see *perestroika* as a revolution from above are only partly right. The history of the rock community demonstrates how youth has forced the state again and again to compromise. Those who see the Soviet Union as totalitarian focus only on narrow issues, however important, and fail to see broader social forces (such as youth) at work. Whereas it was relatively easy to suppress a relatively small dissident movement in literature, the attempt to suppress rock music never stood a chance of succeeding, despite the huge effort and cost invested. Imagine how many rubles were wasted in jamming the pop programmes of Western radio stations.

2. The lack of widespread, overtly expressed discontent during the Brezhnev years was not, at least for youth, the result of any atomisation of society. It reflected a growth in counter-culture, which provided an alternative to active protest. Rather than risk confrontation at a time when it was weak, the state chose to ignore the evidence before it and saw counter-culture such as that expressed in the rock community in terms of isolated, localised groups.

For both those concerned about the health of society and those whose main interest was the preservation of privilege, the state of society was every bit as threatening to stability as the state of the economy. In this way broader social forces gave rise to the conditions in which *perestroika*, or revolution from above, could be contemplated and implemented.

3. The form of counter-culture examined here, the rock community, adopted a strategy of disassociation which has been described here as a rejection of those aspects of official norms and ideology that are stressed most prominently by socialising agencies. Members of the counter-culture, and of many other sectors of society, may express their alienation from official values through drug and alcohol abuse. Legislation is clearly no answer to such problems. The experience of the West demonstrates this. Disassociation represents a breakdown in communication between governors and governed, and the state urgently needs to build bridges if *perestroika* is to be successful.

Nowhere is the link between state and individual weaker or more crucial than with youth. So the leadership as a whole is seeking to understand youth and is yielding to those demands that can be met without threatening internal stability. The muted reaction by youth up to now shows how much further the leadership has to go. It is not helped by those within it who are opposed to *perestroika*. As in the West, a single incident or regressive newspaper article can be seen as the beginning of a backlash for which there have been many precedents. Many young people, who are particularly suspicious of the authorities, feel vulnerable and unsure exactly how to respond. 'More action and faster' is the principal youth message which conflicts with the more gradual evolution of *perestroika*. This problem too will have to be resolved.

4. Given the nature of the forces that gave rise to *perestroika*, largely a reaction to acute social and economic stagnation, any setbacks should be seen in their true light, as despairing attacks by a retreating army. The study of minutiae in the present climate gives a misleading picture. *Perestroika* has already led to great unpredictability

and, as it deepens, the consequences are even less forseeable. Kremlinology should not be a major tool in the future study of the Soviet Union.

5. The rock movement has demonstrated to the Soviet leadership that a section of youth can be given responsibility and freedom without baneful effects on society. There are many youth groups within society that must worry the leaders. The sight of young fascists making Sieg Heil signs in Moscow on Hitler's birthday is an intolerable affront to most Soviet people. The authorities are trying to understand even these youths, but they will have to take action that will certainly antagonise a section of the young. A general atmosphere of toleration and the removal of all restrictions on autonomous activity are, as has occurred in the West, going to unleash negative as well as positive forces, which will have to be examined and dealt with as they arise. If the authorities need to harness the positive forces (which is a *sine qua non* of development), general toleration, patience and encouragement of young people are essential.

Notes

1. My own conversations with Soviet students have confirmed the analysis of the Komsomol made in Chapter 2.
2. *Literaturnaya gazeta*, 15 October 1986, p. 8.
3. For a comprehensive history of jazz in the USSR see Starr, S. F., *Red and Hot: the Fate of Jazz in the USSR, 1917–1980* (Oxford: Oxford University Press, 1983).
4. Troitsky, A., *Back in the USSR* (London: Omnibus Press, 1987).
5. Pond, I., 'Features of Soviet Pop'. Paper delivered to a UNESCO Conference of Pop Sociologists in Delhi, July 1987, p. 4.
6. *Muzykalnaya zhizn*, 1987, no. 6.
7. Pond, 'Features of Soviet Pop (note 5), p. 3.
8. Starr, *Red and Hot* (note 3), p. 291.
9. Ibid., p. 297.
10. Ibid., p. 300.
11. *Literaturnaya gazeta*, 15 October 1986, p. 8.
12. Bright, Terry, 'The Soviet Crusade Against Pop,' in *Popular Music, Vol. 5, Continuity and Change* (Cambridge: Cambridge University Press, 1985), p. 127.
13. Ibid., p. 124.
14. Ibid., p. 127.
15. Interview with Boris Grebenshchikov, summer 1986.

16. From my collection.
17. Interview with Natasha, Leningrad, spring 1987.
18. *Komsomolskaya pravda*, 29 May 1987, p. 3.
19. Ibid.
20. Ibid.
21. Quoted in Troitsky, *Back in the USSR* (note 4).
22. Ibid.
23. From my collection.
24. Troitsky, *Back in the USSR* (note 4).
25. Interview with Victor Tsoi, Leningrad, December 1985.
26. Interview with Leningrad unofficial rock critic Alex Kan, Leningrad, summer 1986.
27. Pond, 'Features of Soviet Pop' (note 5), p. 4.
28. Bright, 'The Soviet Crusade Against Pop' (note 12), p. 142.
29. *Komsomolskaya pravda*, 29 May 1987, p. 3.
30. Title of paper by Bright (note 12).
31. Troitsky, *Back in the USSR* (note 4).
32. *Sovetskaya kultura*, 7 March 1984, p. 3.
33. Pond, 'Features of Soviet Pop' (note 5), p. 123.
34. For these and other examples, see Ramet, Pedro, 'Rock counter-culture in Eastern Europe', *Survey*, summer 1985.
35. Troitsky, *Back in the USSR* (note 4).
36. Quoted in *Rolling Stone Magazine* (New York), 26 March 1987, p. 27.
37. Televizor, *Out of Control* (from my collection).
38. *Sunday Morning Post* (Hong Kong), 12 April 1987, p. 6.
39. For further details see Riordan, J., 'Muscular Socialism in the USSR', *Bradford Occasional Papers* (Bradford: Bradford University Press, 1988). See also Chapter 6.
40. Printed in *Re-Records Quarterly*, September 1985, p. 25.
41. *The Guardian*, 16 March 1987, p. 15.
42. From my collection.
43. Interview with Boris Grebenshchikov, Leningrad, summer 1986.
44. Ramet, 'Rock Counter-culture . . .' (note 34), p. 157.
45. Radio Moscow's North American Service. The 'Tonight Programme', 7 September 1987.
46. From the Leningrad group Zoopark. Printed in *Re-Records Quarterly*, September 1985, p. 26.
47. *Rolling Stone Magazine*, p. 27.
48. Quoted in Troitsky, *Back in the USSR* (note 4), p. 27.
49. *Teatr*, 1987, no. 2, p. 37.
50. By the Moscow group Primus, *Re-Records Review*, September 1985, p. 26.
51. By Kino, *Re-Records Review*, September 1985, p. 26.
52. From what I witnessed during a three-month stay at a Soviet student hostel I am not convinced that only the Westernized youth of the rock community have an unencumbered attitude towards lovemaking!
53. Reported in *Izvestiya*, 28 January 1987, p. 1.
54. From my collection.
55. *Sobesednik*, 1987, no. 1, p. 3.

56. *Literaturnaya gazeta*, 15 August 1987, p. 17.
57. Interview with Alex Kan, Leningrad, July 1987.
58. Ibid.
59. Interview with Victor Tsoi, Leningrad, spring 1987.
60. Quoted in *The Guardian*, 16 March 1987, p. 17.
61. *Muzykalnaya zhizn* 1987, no. 6, p. 3.
62. *Moscow News* 1987, no. 13, p. 7.
63. *The Guardian*, 16 March 1987, p. 17.

4 Rural Youth
Sue Bridger

> I just don't understand why they write about young people who
> stay in the village as if they're heroes. I sometimes read in a
> magazine ... a headline like 'Young people live in the village!'
> And I always think, 'Well, that's clever!' If they'd written, 'Young
> people live on the moon!' then you could understand it, that's a
> difficult business. But why ever shouldn't we live in the village?[1]

For this young woman, returning to her native village after graduat-
ing from an agricultural institute, the countryside had much to offer:
a spacious and comfortable family home, developing rural services
and, above all, skilled work of her choice on an increasingly
profitable farm. For thousands more young people who leave the
village each year, rural life holds no such charms. By comparison with
the city, rural living conditions and the nature of farm work may
indeed appear to demand a kind of heroism of those who remain.

As late as 1960, the majority of the Soviet population still lived in
the countryside. By 1986, the rural population had fallen to 34.4 per
cent of the USSR total. The decline has been by no means evenly
distributed across the Soviet Union. At one end of the scale, the
Central Asian republics with their high birthrates and strong cultural
traditions continue to have a largely static rural population. As a
result, farms in this area are presented with an expanding workforce
which cannot be fully employed in the state sector. By contrast,
northern and central regions of the European USSR, along with
much of Siberia, have experienced intense out-migration throughout
most of this period. The band of regions between Moscow and
Leningrad, for example, part of what is known as the Non-Black
Earth Zone, lost around 48 per cent of their rural population between
the censuses of 1959 and 1979. During the 1960s alone, the proportion of the rural population aged 20–29 in these same regions fell
from between 15 and 17 per cent to less than 9 per cent.[2]

In the late 1970s the rate of migration from the countryside to the
towns diminished considerably. Soviet social scientists ascribed this
development to a range of factors, notably an improvement in rural
living and working conditions and changes in the structure of both the
rural population and the urban workforce. The period of intense out-

migration had significantly altered the demographic structure of the villages in the regions listed above, producing a rural workforce with an unusually high proportion of middle-aged and elderly people. As these groups were far less likely than the young to consider moving to the towns, the rate of out-migration inevitably began to decline. At the same time, the expansion of the workforce in the country as a whole through natural growth had led to a fall in demand from urban areas for further recruits from the countryside.[3]

This decline in the rate of out-migration has not signalled the end of the process as a whole. The decline in the urban birthrate since the 1960s is expected to produce a sharp contraction in the urban workforce towards 1990. As a result, it has been predicted, the urban demand for labour is likely to stimulate a further wave of migration from the village to the town. The majority of migrants to the towns today are young people pursuing their education in urban colleges and universities. Experience has shown that few will bring the newly-acquired skills back to their native village. The loss of their young people to the cities has created considerable problems for farms in areas of high out-migration. With its relatively low level of mechanisation, Soviet agriculture remains far more labour-intensive than that of other developed nations. In 1979, for example, only three per cent of the British and four per cent of the US workforce were employed in farming. By comparison, 20 per cent of the Soviet labour force still worked on the land.[4]

The shortage of young people in Soviet agriculture not only creates immediate difficulties for the farms but has led to fears for the future of agricultural production in areas where young families are rare and children are few. The economist, Victor Perevedentsev, has described the problems caused by migration in the 'typical Non-Black Earth Zone area' of Pskov Region. In 1982, the Region's farms had 5000 livestock workers and almost 11 000 tractor drivers less than the total required to achieve planned production levels. In the five years to 1980, agricultural production in the Region had fallen by ten per cent despite massive increases in capital investment in Non-Black Earth Zone farms. While there was universal agreement that the rural workforce in areas such as this should not be allowed to diminish still further, Perevedentsev felt that the scale of the problem had not been fully appreciated:

> Many people believe that this can be achieved by the retention in the village of greater numbers of school leavers. This loses sight of

the fact that there are often considerably fewer young people reaching working age than the number of people approaching retirement. Let us give a concrete example. In 1982 there were four young people in the eighth form of the 'Zarechensky' state farm secondary school, Novorzhev District, Pskov Region. Of these, two intended to go to agricultural technical college, one to an agricultural vocational-technical school and one to the ninth form of a secondary school. As we can see, the level of 'retention' is extremely high. But is it going to produce much when we take into account that 'Zarechensky' has 260 workers instead of the 443 required to carry out the planned level of work, and that a good many of the workers it has are at or approaching pensionable age?[5]

The reasons for the disastrous loss of young workers in areas such as this and the measures taken to tackle migration will be the focus of this chapter.

WORKING CONDITIONS

The major factor in the decision of most young people to remain on the land is the availability of skilled work in acceptable conditions. With the slow expansion of the service sector in the countryside and the spread of rural industry, some areas are able to offer a greater diversity of employment opportunities to young people. For the overwhelming majority, however, remaining in the village means choosing from a limited range of skilled and unskilled jobs in arable farming or animal husbandry. Though agricultural production is becoming increasingly mechanised, working conditions still leave much to be desired and the hours expected of farm workers do not approach the standardised working week which industry can offer.

This, in large measure, explains the colossally high turnover of young agricultural machine operators. Across the country as a whole more than three-quarters of trained tractor and combine drivers gave up farmwork every year during the 1970s. Because of staff shortages, shift work is rarely an option for the farms to consider. As a result, the working day, in summer especially, may well extend to fill the hours of daylight, and sometimes beyond, seven days a week. A journalist visiting a Saratov Region farm in the spring of 1987 was assured by the chairperson of the trade union committee that machine operators worked a standard day of ten hours in summer, seven hours in winter. As she caustically commented, 'Later it turned out that "seven hours" meant from seven in the morning to seven at night, and even longer in summer.'[6]

In addition, the press receives regular complaints from machine operators about the poor quality of agricultural machinery and, hence, the loss of time and earnings produced by mechanical break-downs. As young, inexperienced drivers are more likely to be assigned older machines, this is a problem which hits them particularly hard. It has also been admitted that levels of vibration, dust and fumes to which machine operators are exposed regularly exceed approved levels. With their technical training behind them, it is not difficult to see why young men in their thousands prefer to take their skills to the factories.[7]

Women are conspicuous by their absence from work on agricultural machines. The heroic figure of the woman tractor driver building socialism on the collectives or bringing in the harvest through the harshest years of the war has proved such a potent image that it still remains part of popular myth, in the West at least, about sex equality in the USSR. In reality, women have never accounted for more than eight per cent of Soviet tractor and combine drivers, except at the height of the Second World War and in its immediate aftermath. At no time since the late 1950s have women formed more than one per cent of Soviet agricultural machine operators. While much is made of the poor condition of farm machinery in an effort to explain this phenomenon, and, without doubt, the hours of the job have little to recommend them, there are clearly other factors at work. Young women are not encouraged to train for this work, may well be refused entry to college if they attempt it and are likely to face obstruction and hostility from the men who monopolise work with machines. The few women who have found and kept employment in this area are in the habit of describing the work as easier than traditional women's spheres such as dairying or fieldwork. The reasons for this apparently surprising opinion are examined below. In any event, work as a tractor or combine driver is unlikely to be seriously considered by most young women leaving rural schools.[8]

Dairying remains the archetypal form of women's work on Soviet farms today. Despite increasing mechanisation and the construction of fully automated units, conditions in dairying remain far from easy. As many as 200 000 Soviet dairy women still milk by hand whilst a further 400 000 distribute feed manually. Add to this the numbers who are obliged to resort to working by hand when power is cut or machinery breaks down and it becomes clear that heavy manual labour has by no means been eliminated from this area of farming.[9]

The principal source of concern among women in dairying, however, remains the extremely unsocial hours which are seen as an inevitable part of the job on many farms. Dairying in the USSR has traditionally employed a system of milking cows *three times a day*, a method which is still in widespread use. A change to milking twice a day and the introduction of shift work to reduce dairy women's hours is favoured by the Ministry of Agriculture and the agricultural trade unions and is steadily being adopted as farms modernise. Nevertheless, a prolonged working day with women on call from before dawn until late at night remains common on many dairy units. Conditions such as these deter young women from entering this work. 'Girls in the Non-Black Earth Zone,' Perevedentsev has noted, 'almost never go to work in livestock units, despite the high wages.'[10] The problem is therefore exacerbated as labour shortages drastically reduce both days off and holidays. Surveys have shown that workers in dairying have less free time than any other category of employees in either agriculture or industry. What this means for women with family responsibilities was described by a Belorussian dairy woman at the National Women's Conference in early 1987:

> We milk by hand and wash the equipment ourselves; we distribute the feed ourselves, also by hand. We are already in the unit by six in the morning and don't get home before eleven at night. There are only short breaks between the three milking sessions to see to the children, to do the washing and cooking. I have a son of 18 and with my work I never noticed him grow up. . . . My friends in the unit have children who are just growing up, and how much they need their mothers to come home on time not completely exhausted . . . It's one thing for me – I've been a dairy woman for 18 years – but you won't entice young women today to Kazimirovka, even with our high wages. They want proper working conditions and to be sure of getting days off and holidays.[11]

The third major area of employment open to rural young people is agricultural labouring in arable farming or horticulture. The mechanisation of arable farming has increased dramatically over the last decade, especially in areas such as sugar-beet production which, in the early 1970s, still relied very heavily on manual labour. Nevertheless, a 1979 estimate still put the proportion of agricultural work done manually at 65 per cent, compared with 38 per cent of industrial work. Labourers in Soviet agriculture are almost exclusively female: in arable farming, market gardening and fruit farming 98 per cent of manual workers are women. Female gang labour is also extensively used in the production of rice and cotton and for general manual work connected with animal husbandry. Fieldworkers are employed for long hours in all weathers on backbreaking, monotonous jobs such as weeding, thinning out seedlings, picking fruit and cotton, and lifting root crops. As the least prestigious form of agricultural employment, fieldwork offers low wages, fluctuating through the year, and periods of seasonal unemployment. Though labouring remains an essential component of agriculture it can hold little attraction for young people with a secondary education. Those who choose to work in fieldwork gangs often do so as a form of temporary, part-time employment while they study for entry to higher education. Not surprisingly, this group of workers is most likely to express dissatisfaction with both wage levels and the arduous nature of the work itself.[12]

A survey of Non-Black Earth Zone farms found that general levels of job satisfaction among young people had improved during the 1970s as agriculture had become increasingly mechanised. Nevertheless, its authors discovered that dissatisfaction increased both with age and with education. Moreover, they found that the majority of young women were unhappy with their conditions of work. This, they observed, had become the prime cause of migration to the cities.[13]

EDUCATION, CULTURE AND LIFESTYLES

With the development of secondary education through the 1960s and 1970s, the educational attainment of the rural population has improved substantially. Despite losing a high proportion of educated young people to the towns, almost half the rural population had received at least a basic secondary education by 1979. The nature of work on the farms, however, means that completing secondary education is more often a passport to the city than a means of gaining skilled employment in the countryside. Among those who seek entry to higher or further education, non-agricultural specialisms are in greatest demand, while those students who begin college courses firmly intending to take their skills back to their native village have often accommodated themselves to city life by the time they graduate.[14]

Not least among the attractions of the city is the diversity of its cultural life. Rural young people are no less preoccupied than their urban counterparts with rock music, discos and the latest films, but opportunities for indulging their tastes are inevitably far more limited in the countryside. Young people complain that there is nowhere to go and nothing to do in villages where clubs are non-existent, in poor condition or badly organised. Observing the attraction for the young of urban-style entertainment, rural officials often bemoan what they see as their inability to make use of all the countryside has to offer. As one remarked ironically. 'A young person sits on the bank of a wide pond and complains that there are no swimming pools or parks in the countryside.' Nevertheless, a 1982 survey of Saratov Region farms found that between 70 and 80 per cent of rural young people regularly travelled to the town to make use of various cultural facilities. [15]

As interest in traditional rural culture has dwindled, folk song and dance has become largely the preserve of the elderly or of those who are paid to ensure its continuation. The boredom which young people express where organised leisure facilities are minimal may act as a further spur to their decision to leave. For some, even tedious unskilled work becomes acceptable where it ensures access to an urban style of leisure:

> We have good housing and good roads, but young people still leave. The village is on the banks of the Sea of Azov and there are 60 hotels on the collective farm's land. Many get themselves jobs as caretakers even, as long as they don't have to work on the farm. . . . There are cinemas and discotheques in the hotels, but there's nowhere to go in our village. [16]

Poor rural living conditions may be a further element attracting young people to the cities. A shortage of shops and services and inadequate medical facilities oblige many rural dwellers to make regular trips to the towns, often for the most basic items. The lack of hard-surface roads across much of the country may make these journeys virtually impossible in spring and autumn when the dirt roads turn to mud: 'If peasants have to send off to town for every necessity they may well think, "why don't I move there for good?"' The authors of the Saratov Region survey quoted above found that the majority of people interviewed made their journeys to town during working hours. They estimated that, for the Region as a whole, the loss of time involved was equivalent to the daily absence from work of over 35 000 rural workers. The financial loss caused both by absence from production and by the use of farm transport for trips to town was estimated at over 145 million rubles per year.[17]

For women who still bear the brunt of domestic labour throughout the USSR, the unavailability of basic amenities and services makes housework considerably more complicated and time consuming than in the towns. As a woman activist from Krasnoyarsk Region recently complained, 'If you look at the official list of services, there are hundreds. But how many of them can rural women realistically rely on? You could count them on the fingers of one hand.' In addition, the lack of a mains water supply to most rural homes and the need to work a private allotment to provide essential foodstuffs for the family place additional burdens on women. The combination of a prolonged working day and these extra components of domestic labour in the village falls very heavily on rural women. In consequence, they enjoy less than half the free time available to women in the towns.[18] Observing the demands made of their mothers' time and energy by rural conditions, young women may have no desire to emulate their experience.

PARENTAL INFLUENCE

The attitudes of parents towards rural life and work appear to be crucial in determining whether their children stay in the village. Rural sociologists, farm managers and teachers in village schools are at one in concluding that parents, and particularly mothers, are the major influence on young people's decision to leave. To some observers it may seem perverse that women deliberately encourage their children to move away permanently, knowing that contact with them in the future may be extremely limited. Others, who have the job of persuading young people to staff livestock units or drive combines, often express their exasperation with what they see as parental obstruction of their work. Where teachers and farm officials attempt to appeal to a sense of patriotism and local pride in young Komsomol members as a means of drawing them into dairying, for example, it seems to be parents more than the young women themselves who object: 'Why did you stay at school till you were 18 to go and wade around a cowshed?' 'Go and study in town. You're as smart as anyone else. If they won't give you a grant, we'll feed you!'[19]

Journalists describing such reactions often point out in apparent surprise that the mothers in question are themselves 'leading dairy women' on these farms. It is surely no conicdence that women who have spent their lives toiling from dawn until dusk and often well into the night in dairy units, on the private plots and in their own homes should want something better for their children. Surveys indicate that most rural women want their children to gain a further or higher education and, preferably, to become specialists in non-rural occupations. Their own evident dissatisfaction with the hardships they have endured expresses itself in their protection of their children from heavy physical work and their encouragement of migration whatever the personal cost:

> My daughter isn't like me – I was never so beautiful even when I was young. Do you really think I would let her ruin her hands milking? I don't allow her to do heavy work at home either. My hands and back have already had it with spending my whole life on the collective farm; so let her go and live in town, in a warm flat. I've worked enough for both of us, and I'll go on working to give her share to the state so that she won't be a parasite.[20]

In recent years, growing concern has been expressed both by Soviet social scientists and by rural activists over this tendency to protect young people from hard work. The view has been expressed that when parents adopt an attitude of 'our life was hard, so let's make it easy for them', they may not be doing their children any favours. Over-protectiveness and a failure to encourage young people to do things for themselves are considered to be a cause of apathy, immaturity and what is termed 'social infantilism' amongst the young. Though this is far from being a purely rural complaint, its impact in the countryside may be particularly striking. Where children are no longer encouraged to participate in farmwork in the traditional peasant manner, there remains little to attach them to the land, as this elderly dairy woman observed:

> By the time I was eight I knew how to milk a cow, how to pull flax and reap with a sickle. Sometimes I remember my childhood and wonder whether we protect our children too much these days from farm work. They grow up, become young men and women and they're afraid to approach a cow and don't know how to hold a scythe. But peasant work surely makes a person's heart become attached to the countryside. Perhaps if we didn't protect them like that they wouldn't be so full of admiration for the city. Just like a person you love, it's hard to leave work that you love.[21]

However tempting it may be to castigate parents or young people themselves for attitudes which lead them away from the land, the fact remains that many farms cannot offer conditions which will compete with those in industry. Commentators on the mass exodus of the young from the countryside have remarked that it is no answer for farm officials to make a scapegoat of young people and their families. As the secretary of one of the agricultural trade unions recently observed, 'Farm managers and heads of trade union committees nowadays look, at the very least, naive when they complain about a lack of workers and accuse young people of idleness, selfishness or being spoilt, yet they do nothing to change the character and the organisation of work.'[22] Where young people are expected to sacrifice almost unlimited amounts of time in often desperate conditions on the farms, they can scarcely be prevented from looking with envy to what they perceive as the good life in the towns.

THE 'BRIDE PROBLEM'

As we have seen, the conditions of life and work in the countryside may be particularly difficult for women. In response, traditional patterns of migration have been reversed in the USSR. Until the mid-1960s, most migrants were young men leaving the villages to do their national service. On demobilisation, they would frequently be drawn into factory work in the towns, leaving young village women little choice but to follow them if they wished to find a husband. In the most developed regions of the USSR, the last two decades have seen an ever-increasing movement of young women out of the villages. Today, where out-migration is at its most intense, women are the first to leave and form the majority of migrants.[23]

This phenomenon has had a catastrophic effect on farming in these areas. Not only does the women's departure leave livestock units chronically short of staff, but it also encourages a high turnover of men employed as machine operators: where women are few, even high pay and the up-to-date technology cannot keep young men on the land. This particular consequence of female migration has given rise to its popular description as 'the bride problem'. The May 1987 edition of *Krestyanka* (Peasant Woman) magazine highlighted the situation with a startling cover picture of three smart young men sitting on chairs in a snow-covered village street. Across the picture ran the words, 'There are big changes in the Staritsa District of

Kalinin Region. The villages here have become more cheerful, there's lots of building going on ... It's a shame there are still so few weddings: there aren't enough brides.' Inside, the lead article provided the statistics: on 1 January 1987 in this district there were 1360 unmarried men aged 18–26, a further 300 over 26, but 'only a few' unmarried women. The point was rammed home with a further photograph of a couple dancing in a local club watched by a row of dismal male wallflowers. Across the Non-Black Earth Zone as a whole, 25 per cent of young men who leave the land cite the lack of women as their major reason. It is a situation which has been regularly discussed, though rarely so graphically depicted, in the rural press over the last few years. [24]

The prime cause of such a high level of female out-migration is the shortage of skilled, mechanised work for women on the farms. Paradoxically, as agricultural production has modernised, employment opportunities for women have become more limited and conditions have deteriorated. While the operation of farm machinery remains an almost exclusively male preserve, women are constrained to perform manual tasks of ever-diminishing status. The prevailing sexual division of labour between mechanised and non-mechanised work on the farms has proved to be so intransigent that traditionally female areas of work are being taken over by men with the advent of machines. In sugar beet production, for example, women are almost never trained to operate the machines which are replacing female gang labour. Where factory farming methods have been introduced to animal husbandry, women rarely use or maintain the related equipment. Even in dairying, where over 90 per cent of workers are women, the most highly mechanised units offering the best working conditions are increasingly attracting male workers who view these jobs as an extension of the machine operator's 'specialism'. In recent years, young men have regularly won national dairying competitions through their familiarity with the most modern milking equipment. Though journalists reporting these events for women's magazines treat these successes with considerable reserve, the men can scarcely be ignored as they smile out of the commemorative photographs like uninvited guests at a wedding. [25]

As young women are denied access to technical training or forced to run the gauntlet of hostility from male colleagues if they attempt to take up work as machine operators, fewer and fewer acceptable alternatives are left to them. For women who would like to stay in the village, only the fortunate few are able to find congenial work in offices or in the underdeveloped service sector. The majority are faced with manual work, frequently in appalling conditions, in the fields or in livestock units. In the changing political climate of the Soviet Union today, there is a growing willingness to admit to the less palatable aspects of female employment. The National Women's Conference which was held in early 1987 was organised by the Committee for Soviet Women, a body not previously noted for its championing of the cause of women agricultural workers. In an uncharacteristically forthright speech, Valentina Tereshkova, former cosmonaut and for many years head of the Committee, stated:

> The level of manual work engaged in by women in agriculture is especially high. . . . This is what women workers from the village of Osipovka, Buryat Autonomous Republic, wrote to the Committee for Soviet Women: 'Our work is backbreaking. We have to move sacks of mixed feed weighing 50 to 60 kilos each. We carry manure from the dairy unit manually.' Letters like this come from other regions of the country. How long will women have to work in these conditions?

It is a question which young women answer resoundingly each year through their departure for the towns. Some 80 per cent of young women leaving Non-Black Earth Zone villages give the lack of suitable work as the reason.[26] Through migration, young women have made it clear that a love of the countryside or the desirable qualities of rural young men are not enough to keep them in the village. Without skilled work in acceptable conditions, they are evidently not interested in being 'brides' for the agricultural workforce of the future.

SOME POSSIBLE SOLUTIONS

The response of the farms to the 'bride problem' has been highly varied and uncoordinated. Many areas have looked to the development of rural services or the provision of new housing, together with a steady improvement in conditions in dairying, to keep women on the land. Appreciating that the growth of the rural infrastructure requires both time and money, as well as confidence that ageing villages have a future, a nationally promoted campaign has been run by the Komsomol since the late 1970s. The campaign appeals directly to a sense of patriotism in young women by encouraging them to form

Komsomol youth teams while still at school and agree to work in livestock units for at least a year after completing their secondary education. Publicity for the scheme in the schools generally culminates in a Komsomol meeting with a title such as, 'Our fathers' land is our land.' Teachers and farm officials give speeches intended to inspire those present to stand up and declare, 'I am staying to work in my native village.'[27] The philosophy behind the campaign is to provide sufficient workers for dairy units, not merely to keep them running temporarily, but to be able to set up the shift systems which will encourage women to stay.

Since the campaign was instigated, thousands of young women have worked in livestock units as members of Komsomol teams and it has been claimed that in certain regions, such as the Altai Territory of Siberia, the impact has been dramatic. In view of the continuing concern over out-migration expressed in the press, however, it seems doubtful that Komsomol activity has done more than scratch the surface of the problem by baling out the farms with a succession of temporary workers. Where units have been fully mechanised, however, and especially where a shift system has been put into operation, the improved conditions not only encourage young women to remain in the village but also attract others from neighbouring farms to join them.[28]

The movement of young people between farms in search of better working and living conditions has been inceasingly reported and, indeed, encouraged by the rural press. Information on job vacancies, accompanied by descriptions of available housing and local services, have become regular features alongside advice to individuals seeking a move. This is no doubt intended to encourage skilled workers to move to labour shortage areas if reasonable conditions can be offered rather than lose their talents to the towns. A young dairy woman from Pskov Region, a Komsomol prizewinner, described her feelings about moving to a Leningrad Region farm:

I can honestly say that we didn't leave our native village in Pskov Region because we were frightened of difficulties. We were frightened of something else – indifference. It was nobody's job on that farm to think about young people's lives. All you ever heard was, 'Just wait a bit, wait a bit', or 'Slow down a bit, you want everything handing to you on a plate.' But we didn't want everything on a plate. We just wanted to live reasonably, to feel that we were needed, to see some care and concern. Personally, I would never have had three children in our old place. But the conditions are right here: a flat with all mod cons, shops, services. People understand family problems – what else do you need?[29]

The readiness of young women to move to other rural areas if better conditions are available is suggested by their response to press publicity. The *Krestyanka* piece on the 'bride problem' in Kalinin Region described above attracted over 9000 letters to the magazine. In the first three weeks after publication more than 1000 people, mostly young women, turned up in Staritsa in response to the vacancies described. Though some were evidently more interested in the abundance of unattached men than the state of local farming, others had travelled from as far as Siberia in the hope that conditions would match their expectations. Not all were impressed by what they found: 'Five girls left today,' the receptionist of Staritsa's only and suddenly overflowing hotel reported, ' "You've got a lot of mud here," they said.'[30]

In recent years, some farms have sought to create acceptable work for women by introducing new forms of agricultural production such as fur farming or bee-keeping. Others have developed subsidiary industries such as garment-making, food processing or even the production of souvenirs where traditional local crafts could be revived to supply shops in major tourist centres. The development of rural industry as a means of solving the 'bride problem' was discussed at the January 1987 plenary session of the CPSU Central Committee where it was proposed that rural workshops should be set up on a cooperative basis with urban industrial enterprises.[31] As yet, however, few farms are able to offer industrial conditions which are sufficiently attractive to encourage young women to remain in their native village. Where industrial employment is offered, it may be on a purely seasonal basis, organised to fill the gaps between the months when women's hands are required in the fields.

A good example of this pattern of employment was established on a collective farm in Tula Region as early as 1970. The farm was already suffering from a high turnover of young male machine operators as they followed the women to the towns. The collective farm chairperson had the idea of setting up a clothing workshop for women who would become both fieldworkers and machinists. The first recruits were former village women who had become skilled workers in the Novomoskovsk textile factory. By 1985 some 270 women were employed by the workshop. From November to May they work a standard five-day week as machinists, then from May to June they weed the sugar-beet fields. July is a holiday month, then from August until October the women assist with the harvest and lift sugar beet. The journalist describing their work visited them in October when, after two weeks of rain, the machines had become bogged down in the fields and it was decided to send out the women in these extremely difficult conditions to lift the beet by hand:

> On the evening of 27 October the House of Culture was showing the
> American film, *The Prince and the Pauper*. There were few people there – children, a few old women, women from the canteen. 250 women from the village of Spasskoye had been out lifting sugar beet. The bus had brought them back at five tired and dirty. Their husbands were going round on tiptoe, children were trying not to make a noise. The brightly-lit stone buildings in the centre of Spasskoye were empty by seven o'clock. People were going to bed early.[32]

Where exhausting manual work in the fields remains an integral part of the working year, it seems unlikely that seasonal industrial employment will be sufficiently attractive to retain large numbers of young women on the land. Indeed, in the example cited above, the average age of the machinists was 35. Young women leaving school in the villages look for skilled, mechanised work, stable earnings and an ordered working week, just as their male counterparts do. If they cannot find that in the village they will turn to the cities, even if they know that life there is no utopia.

BETWEEN CITY AND VILLAGE

For young people leaving the village, a shared hostel room is likely to provide their first taste of city life. 'A hostel is a hostel. However well-appointed it is, everything assumes a certain transience, living out of a suitcase – it is not very suitable for family life.' As this journalist's comment suggests, hostel life may be anything but temporary for thousands of young migrants from the countryside. With little prospect of being offered a flat, young couples marry and have children, often being obliged to remain in separate hostels or to attempt to rent living space privately. Cramped communal living or the total absence of a shared family life, perhaps a prolonged separation while the wife spends her maternity leave with her parents in the country, the not infrequent decision to leave the child there in the care of its grandparents, all combine to place a particular strain on migrant families.[33]

At the same time, the working life of those who move to the city in search of employment may be far from ideal:

> There's no hiding the fact that, for village girls, getting to know the city begins in a hostel or a corner of a relative's or friend's flat. Their working life usually begins with the hardest work, where the most strength or patience is needed. You find them on building sites, cleaning the streets and working machines in factories.

The author of this comment might have added low wages and limited prospects to this catalogue of disadvantage faced by new recruits to the industrial workforce. Conditions for migrants in the towns certainly lead some to wonder why they ever left the village. 'There is no life for me in the sewing workshop;' 'you can really breathe in the village,' are comments typical of those who decide to return.[34] Until recently it would appear that young people who left the village were extremely reluctant to go back, preferring to endure disappointment in the city rather than cope with the loss of face entailed in returning home. As rural conditions slowly improve, however, a decision to return is perhaps more easily made, especially where industrial workshops or modern dairy units have appeared on the farms. The chief agronomist of a Lithuanian state farm described how recent industrial development on her farm was luring young people back from the city:

> Some of our fellow villagers are coming back from Vilnius to their native village. Young people are beginning to realise that they can put a lot of their plans into practice quicker in the village than in the town. Every year 40 students sponsored by the state farm study in technical colleges or institutes of higher education. Besides that, we are building four- and five-roomed houses for families – how many city dwellers have that?[35]

Students of migration are becoming increasingly interested in the prospect for encouraging recent migrants to the towns to return to their native villages. Reversing migration, in this quite literal way, has been seen as essential if the problems of agriculture in labour-deficit areas are to be overcome. A recent study of hostel dwellers in the city of Kuibyshev found that between a half and a third of those who left the village between the ages of 18 and 24 would like to return. By the same token, half of those who had been employed in agriculture and now found themselves engaged in heavy unskilled labour in the factories expressed a desire to return to the land. Significantly, the survey found a marked difference in attitudes between men and women. While the men missed the peaceful nature of rural life and the quality of social relationships in the village, the women were highly critical of rural living conditions, housing and the difficulty of 'finding a good job'. The author of the survey observed that such negative views were unlikely to change with time and that they were a very real hindrance to a return to the farms. This survey confirmed the results of an earlier study of migrants to Saratov which found that women adapted to urban life more easily than men.[36]

For many young migrants there is little reason to go back home. The conditions which drive them out of the countryside either remain unchanged or improve too slowly to make a radical difference. As long as farms are unable to offer skilled work in modern conditions, especially for women, young people will go on leaving with the blessing and encouragement of their families. The road to the town undoubtedly leads to success for some: educational qualifications, work of their choice and an improved standard of living. For others, the charms of city life may prove deceptive as their hopes fail to come to fruition. Yet even those who apparently gain all that urban life has to offer may not entirely escape the village. A woman press operator from the town of Kalinin, much praised and rewarded for her work, deputy to the regional council and Communist Party Congress delegate, suddenly remarked during an interview, 'But if you think, I could have had all this in the village. Of course I could. I was a deputy there too, when I was still a girl. So many years have passed, but when I see on the television young women going out milking, it brings tears to my eyes.' As a measure of her own homesickness, she explained that her son, born and bred in Kalinin, spent all his holidays with their relatives in the countryside and planned to work there after his national service.[37] Like this woman's story, the bare statistics of migration mask many more personal histories tinged with regret, almost with a sense of longing, for the landscape in which their authors grew up. The late Vasily Shukshin, writer, actor and film director whose work focused on the complex relationship between town and country, eloquently summed up the phenomenon:

As I approached 40, I could see that I wasn't completely urbanised, but that I was no longer a villager either. It was a dreadfully uncomfortable situation. You aren't even between two stools – it's more like having one foot on the shore and the other in the boat: not to sail is impossible, but sailing seems terryifying.[38]

It is an experience which thousands of rural young people share as they struggle to adjust to a new life in the city. As first generation town dwellers, like migrants the world over, they remain a people caught between two cultures.

Notes

1. *Krestyanka*, 1984, no. 12, p. 3.
2. *Narodnoye khozyaistvo SSSR v 1980 g.* (Moscow: Statistika, 1981, p. 7); *Narodnoye khozyaistvo SSSR v 1985 g.* (Moscow: Statistika, 1986, p. 5); *Itogi vsesoyuznoi perepisi naseleniya 1970 goda* (Moscow: Statistika, 1972–4) vol. 2, table 4; *Vestnik statistiki*, 1979, no. 5, pp. 69–73).
3. Perevedentsev, V. I., 'Migratsiya naseleniya i razvitie selskokhozyaistvennovo proizvodstva', in *Sotsiologicheskie issledovaniya*, 1983, no. 1, pp. 58–9; Rybakovsky, L. L., 'O migratsii naseleniya v SSSR', in *Sotsiologicheskie issledovaniya*, 1981, no. 4, p. 11.
4. Moiseyenko, V. M., 'Migratsiya i molodyozh', in Vasileva, E. K. (ed.), Sovetskaya molodyozh: demografichesky aspekt (Moscow: Prosveshchenie, 1981,pp. 94–5); International Labour Office, *1981 Yearbook of Labour Statistics* (Geneva, 1981, table 3B; Perevedentsev, pp. 58–9).
5. Perevedentsev, 'Migratsiya . . .' (note 3), pp. 57–8.
6. Ivanova, R. K., *Sblizhenie sotsialno-ekonomicheskikh uslovy zhizni trudyashchikhsya goroda i sela* (Moscow: Mysl, 1980, p. 27); Logvinova, T. F., *Sotsialnye i sotsialno-psikhologicheskie faktory razvitiya professionalnoi orientatsii selskoi molodyozhi*, Candidate degree dissertation (Moscow: MGU, 1976, p. 18); *Krestyanka*, 1987, no. 7, p. 23.
7. Belikova, Z. F., 'Kharakter i usloviya agrarnovo truda i zakreplenie kadrov v selskom khozyaistve', in *Problemy derevni i goroda* (Tallinn, 1979, vol. 2, p. 80).
8. Arutyunyan, Yu. V., *Mekhanizatory selskovo khozyaistva SSSR v 1929–1957gg.* (Moscow: Statistika 1960, pp. 59–60); Bridger, Susan, *Women in the Soviet Countryside* (Cambridge: CUP, 1987, pp. 28–44).
9. *Krestyanka*, 1, 1987, pp. 17–18.
10. Perevedentsev, 'Migratsiya . . .' (note 3), p. 60; Staroverov, V. I., *Sotsialnaya struktura selskovo naseleniya SSSR na etape razvitovo sotsializma* (Moscow: Prosveshchenie, 1978) p. 235; *Lyudi v gorode i na sele* (Moscow: Prosveshchenie 1978, p. 64).
11. *Krestyanka*, 4, 1987, p. 2.
12. Belikova, 'Kharakter i usloviya. . .' (note 7), p. 78; *Izvestiya*, 1

February 1987, p. 3; Lyashenko, L. P., 'Otnoshenie molodyozhi k selskokhozyaistvennomu trudu', in Zaslavskaya T. I., and Kalmyk, V. A., (eds), *Sotsialno-ekonomicheskoye razvitie sela i migratsiya naseleniya* (Novosibivsk; Ural, 1972, pp. 149–51).

13. Bautin V. M., and Orlov, G. M., 'Sotsialnye aspekty sovershenstvovaniya usloviy truda selskikh truzhenikov', in *Sotsiologicheskie issledovaniya*, 1982, no. 4, pp. 92–4.

14. *Vestnik statistiki*, 1980, no. 6, p. 51; Tarasov, Yu. N., (ed.), *Professionalnaya orientatsiya selskoi molodyozhi* (Moscow: Mysl, 1973, pp. 16, 40); *Selskaya intelligentsiya i yeyo rol v usloviyakh razvitovo sotsializma* (Moscow: Mysl, 1979, pp. 110–11).

15. Yelizarev, E. A., Subkov, V. A., and Kutenkov, R. P., 'Faktory stabilizatsii selskovo naseleniya', in *Sotsiologicheskie issledovaniya*, 1983, no. 4, p. 72; *Krestyanka*, 1987, no. 2, pp. 33–4; 1987, no. 1, pp. 14–15 and 1981, no. 1, p. 12.

16. *Krestyanka*, 1986, no. 4, p. 13; 1983, no. 2, p. 17 and 1983, no. 1, p. 14.

17. *Krestyanka*, 1986, no. 4, p. 13; Yelizarev *et al.*, 'Faktory stabilizatsii . . .' (note 15), pp. 72–3.

18. *Krestyanka*, 1987, no. 4, p. 4; *Literaturnaya gazeta*, 17 January 1979, p. 12; Perevedentsev, 'Migratsiya . . .' (note 3), pp. 60–1.

19. *Krestyanka*, 1985, no. 10, p. 22 and 1983, no. 4, p. 15; Evteyeva, N. V., 'Kto i pochemu vozvrashchaetsya v selo', in *Sotsiologicheskie issledovaniya*, 1987, no. 2, p. 63.

20. *Krestyanka*, 1986, no. 6, p. 27; *Molodoi kommunist*, 1977, no. 9, p. 86.

21. *Krestyanka*, 1983, no. 5, p. 1; Vasileva, *Sovetskaya molodyozh* . . . (note 4), pp. 9–10.

22. *Krestyanka*, 1987, no. 1, p. 17.

23. Zaslavskaya, T. I., and Muchnik, I. B., *Sotsialno-demograficheskoye razvitie sela. Regionalnyi analiz* (Moscow: Mysl, 1980), pp. 109–11; Perevedentsev, 'Migratsiya . . .' p. 60.

24. *Krestyanka*, 1987, no. 5, pp. 1–5; *Selskaya nov*, 1984, no. 3, p. 14.

25. Volynkina, L. M., *Ispolzovanie zhenskovo truda v kolkhozakh Kostromskoi oblasti*, Candidate degree dissertation (Moscow: MGU, 1976), no. 12, pp. 45, 99, 108; *Krestyanka*, 1981, no. 4, p. 14; 1978, no. 12, p. 4 and 1985, no. 11, p. 2.

26. *Izvestiya*, 1 February 1987, p. 3; *Selskaya nov*, 1984, no. 3, p. 14; Evteyeva, p. 64.

27. *Krestyanka*, 1985, no. 10, p. 20.

28. Vasileva, *Sovetskaya molodyozh* . . . (note 4), p. 96; *Krestyanka*, 1987, no. 5, p. 11 and 1987, no. 4, p. 23.

29. *Selskaya nov*, 1984, no. 7, p. 28 and 1987, no. 7, p. 20.

30. *Krestyanka*, 1987, no. 8, pp. 10–11.

31. *Krestyanka*, 1987, no. 5, p. 4; *Sovetskaya Rossiya*, 24 August 1982, p. 2.

32. *Krestyanka*, 1985, no. 2, p. 5; *Selskaya nov*, 1984, no. 3, pp. 14–16.

33. *Krestyanka*, 1983, no. 4, p. 14; *Pravda*, 29 September 1986, p. 7.

34. *Selskaya nov*, 1984, no. 3, p. 16 and 1984, no. 7, p. 29; *Krestyanka*, 1985, no. 3, p. 22.

35. *Krestyanka*, 1987, no. 4, p. 4; Staroverov, V. I., *Gorod ili derevnya* (Moscow: Prosveshchenie, 1972), p. 55.
36. Evteyeva, 'Kto i pochemu . . .' (note 19), pp. 62–3; Perevedentsev, 'Migratsiya . . .' (note 3), p. 59; Yalalov, A. F., 'Adaptatsiya selskikh migrantov k gorodskomu obrazu zhizni', in *Sotsiologicheskie issledovaniya*, 1982, no. 4, p. 115.
37. *Krestyanka*, 1983, no. 4, p. 14; Yalalov, 'Adaptatsiya . . . (note 36), p. 116.
38. *Sovetskaya kultura*, 1 March 1977, p. 6.

5 The Political Socialisation of Schoolchildren

Friedrich Kuebart

INTRODUCTION

School is regarded by Soviet political leaders as the most important agent of political socialisation. First, it encompasses practically all young people for an extended period of time during their most formative years and, second, the contents of teaching and the school's organisation and activities can be largely prescribed and controlled by the authorities and geared to the objectives of political socialisation as envisaged by the Communist Party. In fact, the school is even assigned the role of combining and coordinating the efforts of other agents of socialisation, such as the family and youth organisations, in order to reinforce them or to counteract potentially dysfunctional influences, thus attempting to control the whole complex process of the political and moral upbringing of school-age children.

Within the school, formal political socialisation occurs in particular through instruction in the relevant subjects, such as history, social studies, literature or other subjects that directly or indirectly impart political knowledge. Providing we ignore the implications of the 'hidden curriculum', it seems that school instruction which is mainly confined to verbal communication and to the cognitive sphere is of limited relevance to the development of communist awareness. This is particularly true with regard to the overriding goal of turning knowledge into conviction, attitudes and behaviour, a realisation which is also reflected in the goals for the improvement of the political socialisation process within the school set by the guidelines for the school reform laid down in 1984. It is worth remembering that the school reform stemmed from a plenary session of the CPSU Central Committee in June 1983, devoted to problems of Party propaganda and the improvement of ideological work. Thus, the reason for embarking on the reform can at least be partly explained as a reaction to shortcomings in school political socialisation work as perceived by the Soviet leaders of the time. In fact, these had, for some time, been voicing their concern about 'negative' attitudes among young people, such as 'political naivity', excessive consumerist orientations and a lack of devotion to public or state interests.[1]

One of the major problems the reform was to deal with was young people's attitudes towards manual labour, which was not in tune with the demands of the labour market despite a stepping up of vocational training efforts after 1977 to encourage school leavers to choose a blue collar job in industry. The 'correct' choice of a career from the point of view of the demands of the employment system is regarded as embodying citizenship attitudes and proof of patriotic consciousness. The inculcation of a work ethic is thus an aspect of political socialisation and it is to be advanced through the school reform by making labour and vocational training mandatory for all pupils at school.

The second problem, which is at the root of the reform, is the susceptibility of Soviet youth to Western influences in their value orientations and attitudes. As Gorbachov's immediate predecessor, Chernenko, warned at the June 1983 plenum, the enemies of the Soviet Union constantly attempt to take advantage of 'particular traits in the psychology of Soviet youth.'[2] These concerns were heightened by developments in international relations and growing political tensions between the two super-powers. The reform guidelines explicitly emphasise this aspect[3] and urge schools to counteract such influences by making youth immune to 'alien' values against which it can no longer be shielded. This is to be achieved by an intensification of the political and ideological upbringing function of the school. In most instances the reform goes no further than demanding 'improvement' of existing practices. Since there seems little sense in attempting to give a necessarily sketchy overview of the multi-faceted problems of political upbringing and socialisation in Soviet schools, this chapter will be confined to looking somewhat more in depth at a few areas of political socialisation that seem to be of special importance within the framework of the current reform.

MILITARY-PATRIOTIC EDUCATION

Among the moral values to be inculcated in the young Soviet citizen by the formal political socialisation efforts of the school, Soviet patriotism plays a major role alongside a communist attitude to labour. Since the 1960s patriotism has been closely linked to programmes of pre-military and para-military education so that, as a component of communist upbringing, it is generally termed 'military-patriotic' education.

A Soviet author has defined military-patriotic education as 'systematic educational and organisational work based on the principles of Marxism-Leninism directed at strengthening the unity of the armed forces and the people, and at promoting qualities of patriotism and internationalism among Soviet citizens, and which is to supply them with the knowledge, ability and skills required for fulfilling the sacred duty of defending the motherland.'[4]

The point of military-patriotic education in the school is to influence the 'feelings, will, mind and physical development of pupils' in order to teach them attitudes and knowledge 'necessary for defending their homeland and the other countries of the socialist community and for providing international assistance to young developing countries in their struggle against reactionary forces of imperialism.'[5]

Military-patriotic education is a process which begins in preschool education and extends through every stage of the education system. It permeates all areas of teaching and is present everywhere in school life and extra-curricular activities. There is no doubt that patriotism is also one of the values which receives most reinforcement in pupils' home environment, particularly as a result of unforgotten experience by adults during the Second World War, memories of which are also kept alive by Party propaganda, films and public symbols such as memorials.

Military-patriotic education enters every single subject at school. Evidence of it can even be found in the curricula for mathematics and the science subjects as well as in labour training, which emphasises work as a patriotic duty and attempts to teach values, such as discipline and performance of one's duties, which play a central role in military education. But it is primarily the ideologically biased subjects within the curriculum which are allotted the task of military-patriotic and internationalist education, their content directly reflecting this task. This applies especially to history which teaches a view focusing on the defence of the country – especially of Russia – against foreign aggression from the Middle Ages to the Great Patriotic War (1941–45), and emphasising the heroism of the Soviet people and the army. It also stresses the economic reconstruction achievements both of the 1920s and 1930s and of the post-Second World War period with all the sufferings and privations this entailed, in order to produce a feeling of patriotic pride. From the very first lesson, the teaching of literature and the arts also includes these topics and deals with them emotionally. The pre-military training which takes place in senior classes finally links up the inculcation of patriotic values with the teaching of military knowledge and basic skills, preparing male youths for the next stage of socialisation in the ranks of the armed forces.

School extra-curricular work is concerned with a great variety of activities dealing with military-patriotic themes. The organisers of this work are primarily the youth organisations, the Octobrists aged 7–9, the Pioneers (9–14) and Komsomol (14–28), in collaboration with the school. From the rituals of the youth organisations certain military or proto-military forms of expression already have a long tradition in the schools. In the mid-1960s the 'Nationwide excursions to places of revolutionary, work and military glory' started up, since when millions of pupils have visited the battlefields of the Civil War (1918–21) and the Second World War (1941–45) or to other places of patriotic significance. The 'Red Scouts' movement is especially concerned with the investigation and protection of historical evidence of these events. It erects memorials, investigates the whereabouts of those who took part, records reminiscences of survivors and collects exhibits for school museums or for the more modest 'rooms of glory' which are to be found in nearly every school.

Regular meetings with ex-service personnel and veterans of social-ist construction are intended to give pupils the feeling of historical continuity, to help them gain an idea of the sacrifices and suffering which have formed the older generation but cannot be directly relived by the youth of today. These 'days or lessons of fortitude', which are often linked to historical memorial days, have shown, however, that the 'barriers of time' make it increasingly difficult for the veterans to be understood by today's pupils with their interest in the present rather than in the heroic past.[6]

Millions of children from the age of ten are also involved in the para-military summer camps and in the military sports games *Zarnitsa* (Summer Lightning) for 10–14 year olds and, since 1972, *Orlyonok* (Young Eagle) for 15–17 year olds. These are run by the Pioneer organisation and the Komsomol respectively in collaboration with the nationwide civil defence organisation, *DOSAAF*. The pupils are instructed in a variety of military related skills and drill and improve their physical fitness, and they are encouraged to complete the norms of the fitness programme 'Ready for Labour and Defence' (*GTO*).

Finals on a nationwide level are held at the end of the school year, generally in one of the 'hero cities' (Moscow, Leningrad, Kiev), and are much publicised events.[7]

Moreover, participating in the games familiarises the pupils with the army and its requirements on an emotional level and thus serves (for the boys) as preparation for military service. From an official point of view the games are of great importance for the development of the pupils' social activities and for the organisation and control of their leisure time. In everyday school life, however, they compete with numerous other measures and activities, with the organisation of which the schools and youth organisations are overloaded. For this reason it is only a small proportion of pupils that regularly takes part in these games; the Central Committee of the Komsomol together with the USSR Ministry of Defence and other agencies felt obliged to remind schools in a special decree that participation in the game *Orlyonok* was compulsory.[8] On close inspection what appears to be the inclusion of all young people – officially, mention is frequently made of 28 million participants – proves to be a net with many holes.

The key element of military-patriotic education at school is the course 'basic military training', which is taught in the ninth and tenth classes of the general secondary school (as well as in the 15+ technical colleges) with a total of 140 hours. The subject in its present form was introduced as a result of the Compulsory Military Service Law of 1967. The reduction of the period of active army service to two years had to be compensated for by the schools, so that this subject was primarily based on military necessity. At the same time, it presented an opportunity for complementing the system of political socialisation in the schools. The course programme of basic military training stresses the transmission of values such as discipline, order and obedience, which are regarded as relevant not merely from a military, but also from a civilian point of view. To this extent the subject fitted into the schools' tasks of socialisation as set by universal education (up to the age of 17), which was being extensively introduced from the late 1960s. The objectives of basic military training partly coincide with the general goals of political and moral upbringing at school, thus providing an additional means of achieving them. This is intended to teach the following:

1. Knowledge of Soviet defence policies and the global political situation influencing them, as well as of their ideological premises and the role allotted to the Soviet Armed Forces,

2. Pride in the Soviet homeland, its economic and cultural achievements and popular heroism, notions which are to arouse a
willingness to continue this work,
3. Political-ideological vigilance and willingness to defend communist ideals actively, hatred of the imperialist class enemy,
4. Mental and physical preparedness to do military service in the
Armed Forces and, in particular, a willingness to take up the
career of a serving soldier.[9]

The introduction of the new subject was originally fraught with
organisational problems, in so far as retired and reserve officers had
to be employed as so-called military instructors (*voenruki*), most of
whom had no teaching experience. However, during the 1970s the
subject was established throughout the USSR, even in the non-
Russian schools of Republics where it was to fulfil an additional
function: instruction in this subject is always in Russian so that pupils
at least become familiar with the military terminology of the armed
forces, which is to reduce friction when they have to adapt to the
conditions of military service.

In the wake of curriculum reform in the early 1980s a broad
assessment of performance of pupils was carried out in Moscow
schools. As far as military training was concerned the published
results contained few details. Nevertheless, they provided an interesting insight into the problems of political and military socialisation in
Soviet schools.[10]

The investigation shows that military instruction has not succeeded
in giving all pupils a clear idea of Soviet defence policies. The
ideological foundations of military policy and Lenin's statements on
the country's defence apparently remained too abstract for many
pupils and failed to have a motivating effect on their attitudes to
military service; they did not seem to view the world's military
situation as so threatening to make them take a particular interest in
it. Apart from gaps in pupils' knowledge, the examiners deplored the
standard of drill in many schools and failed to note a correct attitude
to military order and discipline – an indication of the unpopularity of
drill among pupils, which was also expressed in the lax way they were
found to behave towards instructors.

An inquiry conducted in the 1970s by Yefimov and Deryugin – one
of the few empirical studies published so far on the attitudes of young
people of pre-draft age[11] – suggests that pre-military training is
unable to produce an entirely positive image of military service

among this age group. It appears again to be military discipline and the necessity of submitting to orders that puts most of them off – 42.2 per cent of those polled gave answers to this effect – while 20.8 per cent were more afraid of the physical strain.[12] However, the great majority (86.5 per cent) did recognise the 'social importance and necessity' of military service.[13]

At the beginning of the 1980s, when international political tension was growing, Soviet leaders became increasingly concerned about lack of moral preparedness for national defence among Soviet youth. This was considered to be due to young people's consumerism and interest in Western lifestyles and youth culture. Top ranks of the armed forces criticised young people's underestimating the danger of war and growing pacifist tendencies. Marshal Ogarkov, then Chief of Staff of the Soviet Armed Forces, accused young people of having a 'somewhat simplified' view of war and peace. Owing to their lack of experience, they regarded peace as always good and war as always bad; he called for a 'decisive struggle' against 'elements of pacifism'.[14] Counter-measures, including Komsomol-organised counter-propaganda work and peace campaigns, were to counteract influences that might spread from the Western peace movement and to prevent the peace discussion among young people in the GDR from reaching the Soviet Union. The 'Peace March' of Soviet youth organised in the early 1980s after the 19th Komsomol Congress, together with other anti-war actions, was intended to channel the peace debate so that it was entirely directed against 'imperialism's' alleged preparations for war.[15]

This highlights a dilemma of political socialisation in Soviet schools which entails the demands for patriotic military training, on the one hand, and the officially propagated support of peace policies, on the other. Moreover, the pupils are confronted in class with peace issues of a more general character in a variety of ways; for instance, textbooks or literary works and even war literature may have effects not conducive to their enthusiasm for military matters.[16] It is also necessary to take attitudes of teachers into account. In an investigation of the results of history instruction, teachers were reproached for putting too much emphasis on love of peace as the main characteristic of Soviet foreign policy and for neglecting aspects of national security and the need to strengthen its defence position and spirit.[17] Thus, pupils can be exposed to conflicting or at least ambivalent values and it may seem difficult for them to steer their way in the direction suggested by the school's official goals for political socialisation.

SCHOOL RITUALS AND STATE SYMBOLS

Since the 1960s the Soviet leadership has been going to great lengths to create a homogeneous system of new 'socialist' rituals based on typically Soviet traditions and occasions, rituals which are to replace traditional holidays and ceremonies rooted in religious origins.[18] The new rituals have been specifically directed toward the various areas and cycles of life, right through from family life and 'initiation ceremonies' that introduce young people to new stages in life and to their initiation into new social institutions and roles, to rituals of working life and the celebrating of public holidays. They are frequently connected to outstanding historical events and used to encourage patriotic traditions and attitudes which are themselves supposed to serve the social and political integration of Soviet society. From a social and political point of view they form the affective foundation of the concept of the 'socialist way of life', which gained prominence as an ideological slogan in the 1970s. In so far as they have been accepted by the population, they also form a link with people's 'everyday culture',[19] focusing on the social and political norms and behaviour appropriate to social relations in 'real socialism'. 'Ritual . . . is seen primarily as a form of political socialisation, as a way of inculcating the norms and values of the dominant ideology.'[20]

Encouraging the population to accept the new rituals is a task of the school as an 'ideological institution', to be achieved partly by including the younger generation in the preparation of public holidays and ceremonies and by performing the rituals in a way suited to their ages, as well as by acquainting them with the symbolic meaning of ceremonies and symbols of the state. The role of the educational institutions is particularly important when it is a question of introducing and consolidating rituals which are not yet established among the population, that is, rituals which the child does not automatically learn to participate in within the family.

Occasions for school ceremonies are the official public holidays and memorial days. These occasions are generally connected with certain historical and political contexts, such as, for instance, the May Day celebrations and the anniversary of the October Revolution. They must be distinguished from the specific rituals and traditions of the school, such as those to celebrate children's starting or leaving school and initiation into the youth organisations. In addition to these ceremonial occasions individual schools also feature special traditions in the course of everyday school life, many of them serving to foster order and discipline.[21] The assumption here is that celebrating certain events in a solemn way makes them particularly memorable, thus contributing to stabilising the political-social value orientations embodied in their content: 'A colourful, theatrically performed, aesthetically attractive ritual fosters a swift and deep acquisition of political and social ideas.'[22]

The role of ritual in bringing up young people was recognised early on in the Soviet Union. Founded in 1922, the Pioneer organisation, in particular, made frequent use of symbolic attributes such as flags, music, emblems, uniforms and badges, which appeared at their most impressive during marches on ceremonial occasions.[23] It was, however, the educationist A. S. Makarenko who in the 1920s emphasised the significance of traditions for consolidating children's groups and made them a pivotal point for his conception of moral and political education. In those days it was a question of arousing and demonstrating revolutionary enthusiasm and looking ahead to group forms of living in a future communist society, whereas today the focus is on historical events, heroic deeds of the Revolution, industrial reconstruction and the Great Patriotic War as the basis for traditions, not to mention the omnipresent Lenin cult which permeates all forms of education. What remains of earlier attitudes is their atheist or antireligious bias.

The outer appearance, the ways of performing in public and the rituals of the Pioneer organisation are clearly based on military forms of expression. Among these are uniforms and military salutes, marching in columns with drums and bugles, lining up for roll-call. It is regarded as a great honour to stand guard at public monuments on ceremonial occasions and there are now 130 towns where Pioneers and Komsomol members from the 6th to 10th classes permanently stand guard by the Eternal Flame or some monument.[24] While everyday school routine does not always provide an opportunity for large-scale ceremonies, military ritual is often used to great emotional effect at the summer holiday camps.[25]

Many of the traditions of the Pioneer organisation reflect its indebtedness to the Boy Scout movement, the forms and symbols of which were adopted by the Communist children's movement in the 1920s as forms of interaction appropriate to the respective age groups although the content had been fundamentally changed. After the 'canonising' of Makarenko's conception of communist upbringing, military rituals were legitimised as elements of tradition in pupil and youth groups. Since the late 1960s the military dimension of schooling has been stressed even more by the strengthening of military-patriotic upbringing and basic military training of senior pupils.

It is also hoped to create an emotional identification with the political system by means of rituals related to state symbols, for example, the national flag, emblem and national anthem. Since the adoption of the new constitution in 1977 it has become evident that school rituals are paying increased attention to state symbols.

In view of the increasing alienation of young people from the tenets of Marxism-Leninism, the political leadership is now apparently focusing particularly on the integrating effects of state symbolism. Thus, the guidelines for the school reform called for schools to pay more attention both to state symbol and to those of the Pioneers and the Komsomol.[26] This demand is taken up by the newly designed Rules for Pupils, committing pupils to 'know and respect' the symbols of the Union and the individual Republics and to 'perform the rituals embodied in them'.[27] In the revised text of the Education Law this is the first duty mentioned in an elaborate catalogue of pupils' and students' obligations and is designed to make them into 'worthy citizens of the socialist Motherland',[28] a duty that was not present in the original version of 1973.

On the cognitive level, state symbols provide a starting point for explaining basic elements of state organisation and the ideological and constitutional foundations of the political system in a form suited to the various age groups. This applies to work in both schools and youth organisations, starting with the Octobrists (age seven). Even primary school children are to gain an idea of the meaning of state symbols. The emblems of the USSR and the 15 Republics are to provide pupils with a concept of the multinational character of the Soviet Union, and emblems such as the hammer and sickle are to demonstrate how Soviet socialism is based on an alliance between workers and peasants. The historical background to the various symbolic elements, including colour symbolism, is explained to the pupils before they receive formal history lessons to acquaint them with certain basic features of the official image of Soviet history concerning, for instance, the October Revolution, the founding of the Soviet state and Lenin's role as leader of the Revolution. The Soviet Union is represented as a peace-loving nation, while the red flag symbolises its ability and preparedness to defend itself. In this way a first idea of notions such as Motherland or Soviet Union is produced.[29]

The intuitive understanding of these notions also helps connect Pioneer and state symbolism, showing young children they are part of a large unified whole. By learning about Pioneer symbolism they are to reach an understanding of state symbolism and to recognise the significance of historical continuity.[30] In this way they are able to identify with the state on an affective level in the sense of Soviet patriotism, convictions which are to be consolidated and actively demonstrated by senior pupils. Thus, this learning to respect state symbols and to participate in political rituals and traditions is intended to teach the maturing citizen to conform at least outwardly with certain political ideas and social expectations. Traditions and rituals are to function as a link between knowledge and behaviour, creating a degree of identification that cannot be achieved by verbal means, for traditions do not 'enforce opinions or types of behaviour on anyone, they include people in practical actions by means of which ideas and norms of behaviour are accepted without any inner opposition.'[31]

This idea was expressed for military socialisation in the Soviet armed forces, but it can also be taken to apply to the goals of school socialisation. To expect rituals and symbols to have such a direct effect appears, however, to be an over-simplification, ignoring in particular the everyday conditions of upbringing where, as Soviet writers have warned, the performance of rituals often tends to have a counter-productive effect on the desired goals of socialisation.[32] This is the case, for instance, when instruction in rituals and symbols involves rote learning and achievement marks and thus produces feelings of aversion rather than positive emotions among pupils. It is just as true when the schools focus on the number of accomplished 'measures' in order to prove to the controlling bodies how active they are. When military forms are overdone and result in mere drill, as often appears to happen at Pioneer summer camps, they trigger off disciplinary problems and even rebellion among pupils.

Another point of criticism is that many teachers themselves fail to take rituals sufficiently seriously, do not participate in them and simply use them as teaching 'methods'. There also appears to be a widespread tendency among teachers to take over the organisation of ceremonial occasions themselves so that arrangements run smoothly, leaving pupils with little opportunity for active involvement. Two results of constricting pupils' participation, so to speak, to 'symbolic activity' are that pupils remain passive or seek alternative forms of experience with a greater sense of meaning, such as religion. Yet these are the very actions which are to be combated by means of traditions, rituals and symbols.

PUPIL SELF-GOVERNMENT

At least brief mention must be made of pupil self-government as a special means of political socialisation in schools. It is a means that does not aim at operating by transmitting knowledge or by influencing the affective sphere, but rather at promoting active involvement and learning through interaction between teachers and pupils in running the school's everyday affairs. Throughout Soviet school history pupil self-government has been closely associated with the role of youth organisations. Whereas in the 1920s, in the revolutionary phase of Soviet education, it was regarded as the main road to the creation of the new citizen of the socialist state, it became more or less dispensable when disciplinary control of pupils' conduct was finally handed over to the teachers in the 1930s.

On the basis of the decree on the general secondary school of 22 December 1977, the special agencies of pupil self-government were re-activated.[33] Before this, their functions had generally been carried out by the Pioneers and the Komsomol as these already provided the organisational framework for pupils' social and political activity. The new agencies were the pupil committees (*uchenicheskie komitety* or *uchkomy*), which were introduced to the schools from 1978. The purpose of these committees was to involve school students more actively in the everyday activities of the school, thus charging them with a task the Komsomol had been unable to perform successfully.

Leading educationists recommended the *uchkomy* as essential, up-to-date tools for promoting pupils' civic and moral upbringing. They were to provide a decisive contribution to producing the political prototype of the Soviet citizen with an 'active attitude to life' as propagated in the 1970s. They were expected to teach pupils habits of active involvement in running the collective, to train their leadership qualities and to develop their ability to carry out tasks obediently and precisely, thus preparing them for their future role in the economic and the socio-political sphere.[34] The intention was to give the individual schools more scope for designing forms of self-government and structures of the *uchkomy* to suit their own specific situations, to avoid too much regimentation so that they could develop their own forms and traditions for the pupils to identify with.

The practical tasks allotted to self-government in the regulations for the pupils' committees published in 1978 were far more down to earth.[35] The main areas in which the *uchkomy* were to be active were:

1. ensuring that all pupils performed successfully, and assisting teachers maintain discipline;
2. taking over organisational work, for example, arranging school ceremonies or excursions;
3. mobilising pupils for work assignments like cleaning jobs.

Officially the committees were to act as executive organs of the class or school collective, to which purpose several subcommittees were formed – for instance, for teaching issues, organising labour activities, discipline and order, school hygiene – thus providing scope for including a larger number of pupils in their activities. There was, however, no clear-cut demarcation line between the functions of the *uchkomy* and those of the youth organisations, though the Komsomol was accorded a 'leading role' in school affairs. On the whole, neither teachers nor pupils seemed to know what distinguished the functions of the new organs from those already in existence.

The consequence was that many schools procrastinated over the setting up of pupils' committees and, where these did take root, they have turned into little more than auxiliary bodies for the school head or the class tutor who determine their jobs in every detail and control the election of the *aktiv*. The pupils who actively participate in the work of the committees are often faced with the difficult task of promoting the interests of the school and enforcing its norms on the other pupils. This complicates their position in the collective and their relations with fellow pupils, especially when they have to control the others and report on them to the head.[36]

Thus the *uchkomy* have by no means become agencies for articulating pupil interests, although their work was supposed to allow a flexible combination of both strong leadership from above and initiative from below. As pupils discovered, initiative from below was only welcome if it complied with the teachers' views. The overwhelming experience showed that nothing was feasible which was not desired or thoroughly approved and controlled from above. The consequence was a profound discontent with self-government among all except a few activist pupils. This disaffection was underlined, for instance, by the findings of an investigation carried out among 850 pupils in the upper secondary schools in the Moscow and Yaroslav regions.[37] Only eleven per cent of respondents thought self-government was of any value, while the others did not understand the functions of self-government at all or criticised the fact that teachers 'forced' organisational work on them all, as a result of which almost everybody had a task or assignment but did nothing to carry it out.

Both the problems involved in pupil self-government directed and controlled by teachers, and pupils' reactions to it – indifference or inertia – were well illustrated in a discussion between the editor of *Uchitelskaya gazeta* and a group of senior pupils.[38] A teacher had complained to the teachers' paper that in her class all efforts at organising self-government and at getting pupils actively involved were met by indifference. In the ensuing discussion the pupils from the group contributed their own experiences and comments, revealing both their resentment at being treated as immature objects of educational measures rather than as individuals with their own ideas, and their dislike at having to obtain permission for all their activities. They complained, for instance, that all their proposals for improving political information lessons and making them less boring were simply turned down. 'How can you speak of initiative or self-government,' one of them summed up their experiences, 'if pupils are dragged forwards and upwards by their ears?'

Discussions on how to make self-government more effective by ensuring more comprehensive participation for pupils and by dismantling the authoritarian structures governing relations between the school and pupil organisations have raised two main points: one is the position and role of the school head and the relinquishing of 'dictatorial' forms of exercising power. The adverse effects an authoritarian style of government has on the development of initiative and pupils' willingness to become committed have been repeatedly pointed out by experienced educators, though it has been assumed the reasons for this are to be found in the subjective sphere, in the training and ability of the individual head rather than in general social conditions.[39]

The other point raised is the legal position of agencies of self-government. Thus, G. A. Dorokhova, an expert in educational law, has argued that the *uchkomy* need to be given proper rights of decision-making in order to attract pupils' involvement.[40] Limiting them to a mere auxiliary status diminishes their authority and thus their socialising potential. Though the draft of the new statutes for the general school published in January 1987 does not actually mention the *uchkomy* it does concede pupils the right to voice their opinions and participate in decision-making through their organisations without specifying precisely how.[41] The way this issue is dealt with in future could prove to be a touchstone for the effects *perestroika* has on education.

FROM SOCIAL CONTROL TO COOPERATION

Neither the goals of communist education nor its tools have been fundamentally changed by the school reform which tends to emphasise only 'improvement' in traditional methods. However, as the value orientations and lifestyles of the objects of education, the pupils and young adults, have changed, the traditional instruments of education have proved increasingly ineffective. Nowadays Soviet educationists are forced to recognise that this change of attitude has occurred despite all efforts to socialise young people within an ideologically-closed system of values and attitudes and that they are increasingly losing control of the socialisation process.

Under Gorbachov it is part of the style of a more critical public debate on social problems that such phenomena are openly discussed and the question of their social origins investigated instead of being concealed behind ideological rhetoric. One example of the relentless stocktaking of contradictions in the attitudes and values of the present generation of senior pupils is provided by an investigation carried out by O. S. Bogdanova, Deputy Director of the Institute for General Problems of Upbringing, and S. V. Cherenkova.[42] The picture sketched by the two authors of at least a significant proportion of school-age youngsters – they do not, however, give statistical details – has little in common with the official image of the committed citizen and worker and reveals trends extremely disturbing for those in charge.

It is regarded as alarming that the majority of senior pupils do not have any clear moral goals and are neither prepared to stand up for their views in public nor even to divulge them to others. On the contrary, a generation appears to be growing up which is focused mainly on itself and its own problems, which is self-centred and profit-oriented in its relations to its surroundings and other people, and which is indifferent to problems of the community. There is a great divergence between the learning of moral values and the appropriate behaviour.

An example given by Bogdanova and Cherenkova of the attitude of many pupils is their behaviour during *subbotniks*, when all able-bodied Soviet citizens are expected to carry out unpaid voluntary work for the benefit of the community: 'The class waits indifferently at the *subbotnik* until the teacher distributes jobs, some senior pupils do not feel ashamed to refuse the social assignment and when they do get down to work they either fail to complete it or find an excuse for not doing it.'[43]

School and curriculum content likewise leaves pupils feeling indifferent. This alienation from school also means that pupils are beyond the reach of the school's educational efforts – and this includes the socialisation goals set by the Party – or that they only regard them to the extent of superficially conforming to the requirements of school performance, so as not to endanger their leaving certificate. Indeed, many young people do not have any clear idea of what they wish to do after leaving school, not because they lack opportunities but because they have not received the necessary guidance from either school or home.

While sociological investigations of the last few years have identified the gap between young people's moral beliefs (as inculcated by the school) and their actual behaviour to be more a problem of adapting to the reality of working life,[44] Bogdanova's and Cherenkova's results lead to the conclusion that the lack or orientation they diagnose is a consequence of the contradictions prompted by the school between the ideological attitudes imparted by teaching and the actual life experience of young people.[45] The function frequently ascribed to the school of being the prime socialisation agency, which is to control the influences of other forces and to channel them in the desired direction, has always been more a matter of wishful thinking than of reality. In many ways the trend confirmed by Bogdanova and Cherenkova towards an increasing individualisation of personal development and towards a 'further destandardisation of moral growth'[46] – which naturally has a political dimension – makes obsolete the Soviet school's traditional set of tools with its emphasis on the collective, on subordination to the 'leading role of the teacher', close social control and the avoidance of conflicts.

To sum up, concern about young people's lack of enthusiasm for school and their orientation on values differing from those propagated by the Party is by no means new, but their withdrawal into private life and their preference for satisfying individual demands could prove particularly critical in view of the 'acceleration' of social and economic development envisaged by the political leadership under Gorbachov. These are policies that rely on the frequently invoked 'human factor', the commitment and active cooperation of Soviet citizens. A starting point for a new educational approach as envisaged by Bogdanova and Cherenkova is the demand that 'the school must teach boys and girls to think and to act on their own' instead of confronting them with standardised rules for behaviour.[47] The tradition of authoritarian relations between teachers and pupils should be replaced, they argue, by the principle of cooperation. This involves increasing opportunities for independent decision-making and behaviour on the part of the pupils as has been shown in the discussion of pupil self-government. It remains questionable, however, whether teachers as a whole are prepared for fundamental changes in the conception of their role. The principle of 'cooperation' is also – and this is probably not a coincidence – the starting point for those 'innovators' who in the autumn of 1986 published a manifesto for a renewal of the school entitled 'The Pedagogy of Cooperation'.[48] The internal innovations they propound for a 'humanisation' of the school would undoubtedly also leave their mark on the political socialisation of schoolchildren.

Notes

1. See, for instance, Chernenko's speech at the June 1983 plenum, *Plenum Tsentralnovo Komiteta KPSS, 14–15 iyunya 1983 goda. Stenografichesky otchot* (Moscow: Politizdat, 1983, p. 33).
2. Ibid.
3. *O reforme obshcheobrazovatelnoi i professionalnoi shkoly. Sbornik dokumentov* (Moscow: Politizdat, 1984, p. 40).
4. Vasyutin, Y. S. *Voenno-patrioticheskoe vospitanie: teoriya, opyt* (Moscow: Mysl, 1984, p. 30).
5. Katukov, A. M. and Tsvetaev, E. N., *Voenno-patrioticheskoe vospitanie uchashchikhsya na zanyatiyakh po nachalnoi voennoi podgotovke* (Moscow: Prosveshchenie, 1984, p. 5).
6. N. Filin, 'Obratnaya svyaz', *Uchitelskaya gazeta*, 16 April 1985, p. 3.
7. See, for instance, Isaev, A., and Segeev, V., *'Zarnitsa' – pionerskaya igra* (Moscow: Mysl, 1983).
8. Decree of 27 Jan. 1982 'O dalneishem razvitii Vsesoyuznoi komsomolskoi voenno-sportivnoi igry "Orlyonok"', *Dokumenty TsK VLKSM 1982* (Moscow: Molodaya gvardiya, 1983, pp. 69–72).
9. Katukov and Tsvetaev, *Voenno-patrioticheskoe* ... (notes), p. 6.
10. *Analiz znanii, umenii i navykov, uchashchikhsya shkol g. Moskvy. Metodicheskie rekommendatsii. Chast. II* (Moscow: Mosgorispolkom, 1983, pp. 108–111).
11. Yefimov, N. N. and Deryugin, Yu. I., 'Puti povysheniya effektivnosti voennopatrioticheskovo vospitaniya molodyozhi', *Sociologicheskie issledovaniya*, 1980, no. 1, pp. 60–6.
12. Ibid., p. 65.
13. Ibid., p. 64; cf. Jones, Ellen, *Red Army and Society. A Sociology of the Soviet Military* (Boston: Allen & Unwin, 1985, p. 152).
14. N. Ogarkov, 'Na strazhe mirnovo truda', *Kommunist*, 1981, no. 10,

p. 90, and *Vsegda gotov k zashchite obshchestva* (Moscow: Voenizdat, 1982) p. 66; cf. V. F. Sorokin, 'Vooruzhonnye sily razvitovo sotsializma', *Voprosy filosofii*, 1983, no. 2, p. 13.

15. See the resolution of the Central Committee of the Komsomol 'O provedenii v komsomolskikh organizatsiyakh antivoennoi aktsii "Ya golosuyu za mir!"', *Dokumenty TsK VLKSM 1983* (Moscow: Molodaya gvardia, 1984, pp. 45–7).

16. T. Mikhaleva, 'Podrostok chitaet o voine . . .', *Narodnoe obrazovanie*, 1985, no. 11, pp. 51–4; 'Kogda podvig pererastaet razmery dolga', *Uchitelskaya gazeta*, 6 May 1985, p. 4.

17. Goroshko, R. I., Shabunevich, N. A., 'O sostoyanii znanii i umenii uchashchikhsya po istorii (IX klass)', *Prepodavanie istorii v shkole* 1984, no. 2, p. 49.

18. Lane, Christel, *The Rites of Rulers. Ritual in Industrial Society – The Soviet Case* (Cambridge: Cambridge University Press, 1981).

19. Zots, V. A. (eds), *Traditsii, obryady, sovremyonnost* (Kiev: Izdatelstvo politicheskoi litreratury Ukrainy, 1983).

20. Lane, p. 19.

21. For a detailed overview of traditions and ceremonies in everyday school life and on special occasions see Marenko, I. S., (ed.), *Primernoe soderzhanie vospitaniya shkolnikov*. 4th edn, (Moscow: Prosveshchenie, 1980), pp. 135–6.

22. Golovei, V. M., Dubovenko, N. F., 'Mesto i rol sovetskikh traditsii, prazdnikov i obryadov v preodolenii mirovozrencheskoi indifferent-nosti sredi molodyozhi', Zots *et al.*, *Traditsii* . . . (note 19), p. 279.

23. See, for instance, Samuel Harper, *Civic Training in Soviet Russia* (Chicago: Ill., University of Chicago Press, 1929) pp. 69–75, 228–30.

24. 'Uluchshat patrioticheskoye vospitanie uchashcheisya molodyozhi', *Narodnoye obrazovanie*, 1986, no. 11, p. 97.

25. For details, see Kabush, V. T., *Pionerskie simvoly, ritualy, traditsii*, 2nd edn (Minsk: Narodnaya asveta, 1985) pp. 161–3.

26. *O reforme* (notes), p. 48.

27. 'O tipovykh pravilak dlya uchashchikhsya . . .', *Byulleten Ministerstva prosveshcheniya SSSR*, 1985, no. 8, p. 32.

28. *Vedomosti Verkhovnovo Soveta SSSR*, no. 48, 27 November 1985, p. 794.

29. Mysova, L., 'Ispolzovanie gosudarstvennoi simvoliki v vospitatelnoi 'rabote', *Vospitanie shkolnikov*, 1986, no. 6, pp. 13–16; N. P. Ivanova, 'Formirovanie predstavlenii o gosudarstvennykh simvolakh v deyatelnosti oktyabryatskikh grupp', *Nachalnaya shkola*, 1985, no. 11, pp. 12–15.

30. See also the new regulations for the Pioneer organisation, *Vospitanie shkolnikov*, 1986, no. 5, p. 38.

31. Suglobov, G. A., 'Traditsii i patrioticheskoye vospitanie', *Voprosy filosofii*, 1985, no. 5, p. 53.

32. Kabush, *Pionerskie Simvoly* (note 25), pp. 180, 184; Golovei and Dubovenko, 'Mesto i rol . . .' (note 22), pp. 282–3.

33. 'O dalneishem sovershenstvovanii obucheniya, vospitaniya uchash-

chikhsya obshcheobrazovatenykh shkol i podgotovki ikh k trudu', *Spravochnik direktora shkoly* (Moscow: Prosveshchenie, 1983, p. 31).

34. Korotov, V., 'Aktualnye zadachi dalneishevo razvitiya uchenischeskovo samoupravleniya v obshcheobrazovatelnoi shkole', *Vospitanie shkolnikov*, 1980, no. 1, pp. 8–13.
35. 'Polozhenie ob uchenicheskom komitete v obshcheobrazovatelnoi shkole', *Spravochnik direktora shkoly*, pp. 187–90.
36. 'Uchenicheskoye samoupravlenie', *Uchitelskaya gazeta*, 11 January 1980, p. 1.
37. Solovyov, S., 'Shkola budushchevo', *Uchitelskaya gazeta*, 31 August, 1982, p. 3; 'Shkolniki o shkole budushchevo', *Sotsiologicheskie issledovaniya*, 1983, no. 4, pp. 115–17.
38. Dubrovitsky, I., 'Otvechayut shkolniki', *Uchitelskaya gazeta*, 2 February 1985, p. 2.
39. See, for instance, Azarov, Yu. P., *Iskusstvo vospityvat*, 2nd edn (Moscow: Prosveshchenie, 1985, pp. 70–1, 81–8).
40. Dorokhova, G. A., *Zakonodatelstvo o narodnom obrazovanii* (Moscow: Nauka, 1985) pp. 70–2.
41. *Uchitelskaya gazeta*, 31 January 1987, p. 1.
42. Bogdanova, O. S., and Cherenkova, S. V., 'Sovremenny starsheklassnik', *Sovetskaya pedagogika*, 1986, no. 8, pp. 18–25.
43. Ibid., p. 22.
44. See F. R. Filippov, 'Orientiry sotsiologa', *Kommunist*, 1986, no. 8, p. 124.
45. See also Plotkin, M. M., Shirinsky, V. I., 'Deyatelnost shkolnovo komsomola po mestu zhitelstva', *Sovetskaya pedagogika*, 1986, no. 8, pp. 30–34.
46. Bogdanova and Cherenkova, 'Sovremenny starsheklassnik' (note 42), p. 21.
47. Ibid., p. 23.
48. 'Pedagogika sotrudnichestva', *Uchitelskaya gazeta*, 18 October 1986, p. 2.

6 Teenage Gangs, 'Afgantsy' and Neofascists

Jim Riordan

> We're going to cleanse society of the hippies, punks and heavy metal fans who disgrace Soviet life.[1]

TEENAGE VIOLENCE

In recent years the Soviet media have turned increasing attention to the theme of teenage violence: 'All the papers write regularly about the senseless cruelty of today's teenagers.'[2] The problem is by no means new; but the reporting of it is, as is the screening: a number of feature and semi-documentary films, most notably the Latvian, 1986 film *It Isn't Easy to be Young*, have shown Soviet youth 'warts and all'. As one of the young actors in this film pointed out, 'Youth problems have certainly been around for ages, but they were played down, stifled ... We were protected from knowing too much about ourselves.'[3] Today, *glasnost* is helping to reveal a whole range of phenomena that just a few years ago were repressed: hippies and punks, night bikers and drug addicts, soccer hooligans and muggers, glue sniffers and prostitutes, vigilante gangs and skinheads, Zen Bhuddists and Hari Krishna followers, even Swastika-sporting young neofascists. They may be abhorrent to 'polite society', and have been condemned by leaders from Gorbachov to Archbishop Mikhail of Vologda and Velikoustyug. Gorbachov has spoken of 'a certain section of young people enclosed in its own narrow little world, out of step, or trying to get out of step, with the swift onrush of life',[4] while the Archbishop has written in *Pravda* of the 'moral decay' among teenagers.[5]

Like Western attitudes to AIDS, it is evidently felt that openness is the best policy. After all, youth disaffection from official organisations and values is a widespread and growing problem (see Chapter 2). A number of cities are suffering chronic problems of teenage gang 'warfare', especially in the new housing estates that are said to be 'no-go areas' for many youngsters.[6] But the most intractable of teenage problems appear to be those posed by the new vigilante gangs, the returning 'Afgantsy' and the young neofascists.

VIGILANTE GANGS

The term 'vigilante gang' is a blanket expression for a motley assortment of young people who, disillusioned with official inactivity towards lawlessness and corruption, have been forming their own clandestine vigilante gangs to combat what they perceive as anti-social and, therefore (to them, axiomatically) anti-Soviet behaviour. It would be wrong to classify them all, as one British newspaper has, as 'a uniquely Soviet version of skinhead toughs who attach themselves to the National Front in Britain'.[7] In fact, they differ markedly in their social and political orientation.

Some appear to be responding to Gorbachov's appeal to young people to show initiative in rooting out corrupt officials, bureaucrats, embezzlers and speculators.[8] A thirty-five-strong band of young men from the Siberian city of Novosibirsk has two main targets: 'inveterate speculators and second-hand dealers' and 'officials who abuse their positions'. The band has chalked up fifty-three good deeds and has another fifteen pending investigation. So organised are these guardians of law and order that they keep computer files and were planning to open a Ukrainian branch in October 1986. Once they gain proof of guilt, they destroy the ill-gotten gains and leave the victim copies of incriminating evidence to dissuade him/her from informing the police.[9]

A clandestine Moscow self-styled 'Law and Order' group forces miscreants to help the families of dead Afghan campaign heroes. It also sent four investigators to the Moscow Hippodrome horse-race track where they found,

> Corruption at every step, with bookmakers and money-lenders acting quite openly, fearing no one. A good half of the jockeys were 'bought', races being decided beforehand and profits shared, each jockey making thousands of rubles out of the punters. The management is hand in glove with the criminals and the police turn a blind eye.[10]

Before our local heroes could mete out rough justice on eight of the leading conspirators, one of their members took fright and sent evidence to the newspapers, which brought official intervention.

The awkward dilemma for the authorities is that these gangs regard themselves as good Komsomol members, taking on the mantle of Robin Hood's band (*Robingoodovtsy*) or the author – Arkady Gaidar's *Timurovtsy* – helping the good and wreaking vengeance on the bad. A certain Maxim calls his band 'an informal association of Komsomol members'; a Pskov member of Gang X says the gang's aim is 'to let all scum know they have to deal with us – the people's will – as well as the law'.[11]

How should the authorities react? Are they wrong-doers or heroes? Should the police work with or against them? Some officials admit 'there is no doubt that the groups of noble, I stress "noble", conspirators have arisen as a result of the inactivity and foot-dragging of local police'.[12] Another commentator writes, 'they don't trust us older people and even less the police. So they strive to establish law and order both for their own district and for the country as a whole.'[13] The official dilemma is most evident with the Rambo-style youth cult known as the *Lyubery*.

The borderline between 'noble' vigilante groups and gangs of 'patriotic' thugs is often thin and mobile. While the common foe would appear to be 'people harmful to society', the perception of 'villainy' differs, as do aims and methods. The above-mentioned 'Robin Hood' gangs consist mainly of young people in the context of one locale, teenagers who investigate and punish corruption by relatively peaceful (albeit illegal) means. The Lyubery have more ambitious aims relating to society as a whole and they espouse violence in pursuit of their mission. Furthermore, while the victims of the former are mainly corrupt officials, those of the latter are largely Westernised young people.

The Lyubery impose a strict discipline upon members, requiring initiation tests of neophytes (e.g. beating up punks) and having a hierarchical structure with leaders who are sometimes older ex-servicemen. As a member of 'The Office' (*Kontora*) gang explains,

> We are split into groups, each of which has its own leader. It isn't easy to become a member of The Office ... you have to prove yourself in battle. Show you're smart, obedient and mean.[14]

The name Lyubery comes from the Moscow industrial suburb of Lyubertsy, some twelve miles south west of the capital; its teenage thugs have been terrorising neighbouring urban centres like Moscow, Podolsk and Nakhabino, according to one source, for some 10–15 years.[15] Today they travel farther afield in search of victims (e.g. to Leningrad – some 700 miles away!),[16] and they find imitators in and around many Soviet conurbations.

These male teenage toughs are generally staunchly puritanical: 'They don't drink, smoke or take drugs, and they engage in sport in gyms they've built with their own hands.'[17] Many are dedicated body-builders whose rippling muscles show through their everyday cloth-ing. As one victim says of the gang of four that beat him up, 'all were strong, with well-developed muscles bulging under their jackets'.[18] This obsession with martial arts and body building is well docu-mented, although the Lyubery spurn official sports clubs and build their own gyms in the basements of blocks of flats, their 'bunkers'; they are quite proud to show off their 'vast arsenal of barbells and weights'. They boast of their involvement in 'boxing and weight training, and so on, that make us tough and confident in our-selves'.[19]

The macho obsession disturbs the authorities who regard the 'karate, boxing and senseless muscle-building as dangerous'.[20] The police have raided basements in Lyubertsy and elsewhere, confisca-ted equipment, shut down the 'underground' gyms and tried to channel interest into organised sports clubs under specialist coaches without any marked success.

Like gangs the world over, the Lyubery have their own distinctive uniform and give themselves nicknames. Unlike the 'Westernisers', these latter-day 'Slavophiles' take Russian names, like *Zayets* (Hare), *Utyug* (Iron), *Shkaf* (Cupboard) and *Ryhkly* (Fatso). They are generally clean-cut and wear white shirts and narrow black ties, unfashionable jackets and wide, clown-like, check trousers. Some even have their own way of walking (in a sailor's roll), with hands smartly behind their backs. They eschew foreign slang and even have their own song,

> We were born and bred in Lyubertsy,
> Centre of raw, physical power.
> We know that one day soon our
> Lyubertsy will be the centre of Russia.[21]

The Lyubery are self-appointed guardians of what they see as genuine Soviet values and way of life. Their 'patriotism' extends to trying to intimidate, and cleanse society of, all alien elements, first and foremost followers of Western fashion. As one 16-year-old from

Lyubertsy puts it, he and his mates are against 'anyone who wears chains or foreign badges, has dyed hair and brings shame on our country ... anyone who looks or acts as a protester'.[22] Another young affiliate, in reply to a query as to why he takes the thirty-minute train journey to Moscow each night, says 'we come to beat up punks, hippies, heavy metal and break dance fans'.[23] When asked why he hates such people, another young tough replies that 'We're going to cleanse society of the hippies, punks and heavy metal fans who disgrace Soviet life.'[24]

The questioner had to admit that when he 'first heard that reply I didn't believe it. But when it was repeated time and again, I was left in no doubt'.[25] This is what makes the Lyubery unique and distinguishes them from the housing estate gangs (courtyard v courtyard) of the 1960s or the *besprizornye* of the 1920s – children lost or abandoned during the Civil War, who lived an anarchic and criminal life, developing their own outcast and anti-authoritarian culture.

The principal target of Lyubery ire is the 'Westerniser', the follower of Western youth culture – hippies, punks, heavy metal fans, break dancers – young people whose appearance marks them out as being different. The toughs are also not averse to 'foreigner-bashing' and are said to hang around the big hotels looking for victims. It was the Lyubery who were blamed by the Soviet authorities for roughing up Jewish refuseniks and Western correspondents on Moscow's Arbat in early 1987.

Dialogue with 17-year-old Yuri from a Moscow suburb:

We go to town for a fight. Against the metallists.
Why can't you resolve your differences peaceably?
Peaceably? If that shit were to look normal, maybe.
How do you mean, 'normal'?
'Without their iron chains, hair down to their arses, their painted dreadlocks.
But surely that's an individual's choice to look as he wants. It isn't your affair.
Ha! Individual choice. This isn't the West, you know! Take a ride on the metro ... Cockscomb head. Makes you puke just standing next to them...'[26]

So speaks the 'not-so-silent majority'. Or does it? It is hard to say. At any rate, many Soviet ideologists now accept that it is their own militant moralising in the past that has not only spawned these 'muscular socialists', but is hampering the new democratic openness.

One Moscow gang that calls itself the 'Menders' (*Remontniki*) tries to mend the minds of 'all who act and think differently to themselves'. A Leningrad gang claims to be 'correcting the views of their peers'. As one commentator admits, 'whether we like it or not, the 'menders of men's souls have gained from us adults the licence for moral education of those who stand out from the crowd'. And in a tacit condemnation of the past (and lingering present), he writes,

> Suppression in the sphere of ideas ultimately distorts the ideas themselves and engenders conformists and time-servers, alienates people from independent thinking, brands any fresh idea as alien, which society has to combat by the old 'Cossack methods'.[27]

Well put. Even if it is a bit late. After all, 'to a man all the Lyubery I've met believe in the importance and social worth of their mission in flushing out the punks, hippies and metallists. Yet when you think about it, there's surely no big difference between a common thung and one acting out of ideological conviction.'[28]

The trouble is that for so long the authorities tried to keep out Western mass culture and branded its domestic adherents as unpatriotic riff-raff. As 14-year-old Sergei, a heavy metal fan, complains,

> Do you know who's responsible for these 'cleaners'? Not us, not the punks, hippies or break dancers, but Soviet media. For how many years, for instance, have they portrayed rock as satanism, hell bent on causing violence and pornography? So when they read those articles and hear those diatribes, some young people think the only way to respond is to fight it tooth and nail.[29]

Even now the police are said constantly to harass Western-oriented young people: 'They police stopped me five times in one day to check my papers just because of the way I look, and they didn't talk very civilly either.'[30]

So long-haired Sergei does not bother to complain to the police when he is mugged. Nor did hippy Yevgeny after being halted by five youths on Marx Prospect in Moscow's city centre, forced to his knees and cropped. Either from collusion or, as some suspect, from impotence, the police do not act because 'the hippies, punks and metallists, all Lyubery victims, don't file complains'. As is now admitted, 'Isn't it us that have created a situation where some young people feel the law won't protect them?'[31]

It was police harassment of 'Westernisers' and apparent neglect of Lyubery that recently brought strict instructions from the Soviet

Ministry of Internal Security 'to combat law-breakers, *not* long-haired youngsters with bells on their trousers'.[32] All the same, reports indicate more police success in restraining Lyubery opponents. Like the 500 Moscow teenagers who marched through the city centre one Sunday evening in February 1987 to protest at police inactivity against the Lyubery.[33] Like the 300 Leningrad youths who marched down Nevsky Prospect in early March 1987 in similar protest at the rumoured arrival of the Lyubery (77 protesters were arrested, and two knuckle dusters, two metal belts and two clubs were confiscated).[34] Yet when the police raided basement gyms in Lyubertsy, of the 500 people they registered, only three corresponded with those on the street gang wanted list.[35] Moreover, of the over 200 Lyubery detained in Moscow throughout 1986, almost all were charged with 'infringing smoking, drinking or noise regulations, but virtually none for criminal acts.'[36]

Many victims of the Lyubery are bound to suspect that individual policemen are sympathetic to their self-styled assistants and champions of moral purity. The police have certainly taken drastic measures to avoid street violence and gang warfare. In early 1987, parents in one Moscow district were summoned to schools and ordered to keep their children home that weekend for fear of street violence. There was even 'panic' talk of sounding an air-raid warning to clear the streets.[37]

Fights, muggings and gang battles have become a serious problem in all Soviet urban centres: 'Fights have occurred virtually every evening [between Lyubery and "Westernisers"]. Information from various cities has indicated that similar problems exist there too.'[38]

In almost all cases it is gangs from outside the metropolis, the suburban commuter gangs which descend on city centres, mark off their own 'turfs' or manors, their own cafes and discos. They mug 'aliens' and are even reported to have 'abducted' girls from city discos back to their own suburbs.[39] Some confiscate badges, leather wrist bands, bracelets, even stud denim jackets, soccer scarves and 'unpatriotic' cassettes, which later turn up in second-hand stores. Some are said to rob ordinary people not of 'attributes of an alien culture', but of expensive and fashionable items, on the excuse that they are 'surplus luxuries'.[40] Statistics show that 22 per cent of gang assaults are, in fact, for fashionable Western clothes.[41] Some gangs are said to be run by older 'kings' with criminal records; one such gang boss boasts he can summon over 200 gang members in just a couple of hours.[42]

No doubt, partly because 'nothing like the Lyubery has existed before',[43] rumour is more colourful than reality. But the established facts do demonstrate a serious and mounting problem that the Soviet authorities face as they now try to cultivate a hundred blooms in the new garden. As a Soviet historian explains about the problems of trying to democratise an ossified, despotic society,

> We want to free our young people from paralysing over-organisation, then all of a sudden we run into the problem of the Lyubery ... This side-effect is disappointing and repugnant because no one expected it. But it is real and there is no escaping it. It is time we learned the rules of behaviour in democratic conditions.[44]

A rather bizarre twist to the Lyubery story came in mid-1987, following a speech by the Soviet Deputy Police Commissioner, Major-General Victor Goncharov, warning of youths emulating the gangs they read about in 'sensationalist' press reports. Some periodicals then informed their readers that the Lyubery did not exist at all; the investigative journalist Shchekochikhin had to recant and wrote in *Literaturnaya gazeta* that rumours about the Lyubery had been exaggerated by irresponsible journalists. The Deputy Editor of *Moskovsky komsomolets* declared that the Lyubery were 'something cooked up by certain journalists'.[45]

Apparently some people in high circles were trying to play down any mobilisation of public opinion against the threat posed by the Lyubery. As Boris Kagarlitsky, a leader of the Moscow Club for Social Initiatives, put it, 'the anonymous influential protectors of the Lyubers were one and the same with those opponents of Gorbachov's liberalisation who were keeping quiet for the time being'.[46] Whatever the reason, the curtain came down again, and no adverse material on the Lyubery appeared after the spring of 1987.

THE AFGANTSY: 'RETURN OF THE LOST GENERATION'

The emergence of such 'muscular socialists' as the Lyubery and other unofficial groups partly has its source in the confusion felt by the many thousands of young men who have returned after their harrowing experience in Afghanistan (between 15 000 and 20 000 young men were sent to Afghanistan each year from 1980 to 1987). Battle-hardened and prematurely aged by their service, some

'Afgantsy', as they call themselves, have found it hard to settle back into civilian life and to accept with equanimity the Western youth culture they see around them.

> They talk mostly about the life they've returned to and in which they can't live as they did before . . . They've come back with such purity in their hearts and clarity in their minds . . . These are the people the Fatherland needs most today.[47]

Another journalist, writing in the same youth (and Komsomol-run) weekly, says of these 20-year-olds that 'they have experienced the full horror of war . . . which has stamped itself upon them, changing something within them. They differ radically from their age-mates.'[48] In the previously mentioned film *It Isn't Easy to be Young*, their predicament is called 'the return home of the lost generation' which, for at least one of their number, ends in suicide through disillusionment and disorientation.[49]

One returning conscript, Alexander, says he seemed to have 'landed on another planet. Painted girls totter about, super-fashionable boys meet each DJ's announcement of a tape by a group from "over there" [the West] with squeals of delight, and hiss our Soviet music. Wide-boys in the toilets . . . We are stifling in this dirty little world.'[50]

Alexander tells the story of going to a comrade's wedding and seeing a waitress wearing a jumper with a stars and stripes badge with 'Made in USA' motif (reminding him of the same inscription on the mine that killed his best friend in Afghanistan); an uproar ensued and the police had to be called. Alexander's view of many youngsters is that,

> They've forgotten the real value of life. I don't believe that if it came to it all those girls and boys in their fancy gear with foreign labels would defend the country. It was one such fellow who betrayed us in Afghanistan; we later found out he had been a disco king back home.[51]

Because they find the authorities dragging their feet in tackling social ills, as well as what they regard as anti-Soviet conduct on the part of young people, many Afgantsy are setting up their own veterans associations: the 'Green Hats' (after the hats worn by Soviet border guards), the 'Reservists', the 'Marines' and 'Internationalist-Soldier Councils' which all engage in what their members call 'military-patriotic education of young people'.[52] This sometimes involves meting out rough justice to those who do not share their patriotic ardour and perception of morality.

It is here that they often overlap with the Lyubery. A vigilante gang called 'Waterfall' (*Kaskad*) in Kazan, whose long-term programme is 'to eliminate all groups harmful to society' confesses to having ex-soldiers as leaders and feels it necessary to act 'as in Afghanistan inasmuch as there can be no victory without military discipline.'[53]

When a journalist from the weekly *Literaturnaya gazeta* asked Vadim, ex-serviceman and Lyubery, whether 'the hatred (towards 'Westernisers') was being fomented by ex-conscripts, he was told, 'I saw blood, sweat and tears in Afghanistan . . . We did what needed doing. Never forget that.'[54] But the question went begging. None the less, it is admitted that the Ramboesque teenagers 'will follow the Afgantsy and show an interest in martial arts camps'.[55] Perhaps the fury is understandable when the returning servicemen find themselves taunted by groups that call themselves the 'Pentagon' and renamed their districts 'California' and 'Washington'.

Not a few adults would like to see the returning heroes given their head to try to instil some discipline and respect into dissolute youths. 'Outraged' of Andizhan (Uzbekistan) writes to *Smena*, warning that, 'It is only a short step from fetishisation of imported rags to murder, from striving after an easy life to betraying the country.'

The writer, a school mistress, feels that today's young people need the firm hand of the Afgantsy:

War! Only merciless war on all these things. Instil maximalism in all moral issues. That same maximalism that the lads who call themselves Afgantsy are now displaying, those who have had the whiff of gunpowder in their nostrils and have gone through hell in Afghanistan.[56]

What often irks the conquering heroes, however, is that society does not always recognise the debt it owes them for doing their 'internationalist-patriotic duty' in Afghanistan, and is wary of giving them responsibility to apply their zeal to civilian life. Thus, Lieutenant Vladimir Kolinichenko complains that only two former internationalist-soldiers have been made Komsomol secretaries in the whole of Moscow's 33 districts. 'They don't welcome people dedicated in deeds not words to the Soviet system.' Why? Because, it seems, 'the Afgantsy stir things up, make people do work they're not accustomed to'.[57] From Tadzhikistan comes a letter to *Sobesednik* from the President of an Internationalist-Soldier Club, writing that in the face of official hostility the Club has been forced to set up its own 'Komsomol detachment' – 'it's hard to overestimate the help from the Afgantsy', he says, 'they'll go through hell and high water for justice.'[58]

In the city of Kuibyshev, a seventy-strong group of Afgantsy even took over a district Komsomol committee for a month, calling itself the 'Opposition' (*Protivostoyanie*). They took over because of what they claim was 'neglect of military-patriotic work in the district'; and they appointed ex-army man Valery Pavlov as leader. Surprisingly, the usurpers served out the month without official resistance.[59]

An even more challenging event took place in late October 1987 in Ashkhabad, capital of Turkmania and near the Afghan frontier: some 2000 young men who had served in Afghanistan had a rally and camp, their aim being 'to define ways of improving military-patriotic education of young people'.[60] The rally certainly had semi-official approval, though it clearly came as a surprise to the central authorities. That the objective was not only to flush out 'bureaucrats' was apparent from the statement made by one of the camp's organisers:

It was much simpler in Afghanistan. We knew full well who the enemy was and had to be destroyed. But you can't stick a bureaucrat up against a wall here, or scare home-grown punks and drug addicts with a machine gun. We have to find some other way.[61]

Not all those at the rally shared the disciplined approach of its leaders; reports mention veterans going on the rampage, 'staggering about drunk in their army fatigues, trying to stop buses:'[62] Small wonder that some people are cautious about handing over responsibility to such 'muscular socialists'. As Vladimir Chernyshov, ten years in the paratroops and two years in Afghanistan, admits, 'There are some Soviet as well as Western voices calling us thugs (*golovorezy*).'[63]

It later emerged that the rally had been the culmination of a spontaneous movement begun in 1985, as 'clubs and councils appeared like mushrooms after the rain'.[64] Despite official opposition and unwillingness to help with provision of drill halls, uniforms and combat sport equipment, the 'Young Paratrooper' movement succeeded in coordinating activities and providing all that the state had refused. All the same, the problems the Afgantsy face are daunting: 'Committee work and drill are unending, at home they have to put up with the wife's hysterics because she never sees her husband, at work their workmates murmur about them wanting this, that and the other, at college they are forever at odds with the administrators'. So why do they do it? 'Not for ourselves, but for those whom we left behind.'[65] They now even have their own record distribution system, arranging to post records by such groups as the 'Blue Berets' and 'Waterfall' all over the country.[66]

This tentacular solidarity movement of resistance to what is vaguely perceived as unpatriotic, bureaucratic and effete values and actions is patently growing in size and significance. Where exactly it is heading its own members are no doubt uncertain; for the moment the 'Afgantsy' seem to possess no long-term coherent plans for political power, let alone for the overthrow of the current reforming leadership of the country. All that could alter if aspirations, aroused by Gorbachov's policies, find no satisfaction through their participation in shaping their own and the nation's destiny, and in receiving the attention and treatment they feel are their due. There are already right-wing groups, like *Pamyat*, bidding for their allegiance should they seek an active opposition.

The problems posed by and confronting the 'Afgantsy' are complex and varied. Not all ex-servicemen are agitating for change in the same direction or at the same pace. Like the returning Vietnam veterans in the 1970s, some – perhaps the 'silent majority' – just wish to live quietly, to try to forget; some find the communal comfort and quiet contemplation of religion a boon; some 'escape' through drink or drugs. Few, however, can pick up the pieces of their pre-Afghanistan lives and continue as before. Politically, it is the active vanguard or resistance movement that poses the greatest threat to the stability of society – whether for good or bad in terms of perestroika may well depend on the pace and direction of that process.

What is so unpredictable about the impact on Soviet politics and society of the 'Afgantsy' is that they are acting on a new stage, partly erected by the war, which is providing fresh, unprecedented opportunities for debate, coordinated action and opposition. In the USA, it was incomparably simpler for returning soldiers of various dispositions to find their niche, interest group, community, channel or medium for expressing protest, letting off steam or 'turning off' altogether. As the many studies show, however, few could completely escape from their war memories or discover a panacea for healing their mental wounds. In the USSR today, society is in flux from the old totalitarian, centralised model to a more decentralised, open system that is increasingly providing scope for a range of interests by way of informal youth associations, independent clubs, cooperatives, charities, even extremist gangs and groups that may well facilitate the reintegration process or, at least, offer the 'Afgantsy' a 'safety valve' for letting off steam.

FASCISTS

It must be shocking for the older generation that suffered so much in the war against fascism to learn of the existence in their midst of Soviet fascist sympathisers. Their fury was evident, for example, when they read the letter from a group of anonymous punks from the Novokuznetsk Youth Cafe to *Sobesednik* in May 1986, expressing their spiritual affinity with fascism and stamping on hallowed Soviet beliefs.[67] Predictably, they drew the attention they desired. Probably like many of the 'stunned' Soviet public, the readers who responded made no distinction between 'rock lovers' and punks, on the one hand, and 'traitors' and 'fascists' on the other. As one of the printable replies put it succinctly, 'the whole lot should be shot at birth'. All the same, the journal's editors admitted that the 'punks' had also had their 'advocates' who pointed out the social injustices of Soviet society that 'spawn fascist yobboes'.[68]

Although information is understandably patchy and the scale of fascist influence uncertain, there is no doubt about the existence of fascist youths and adults. A rock group from the Urals town of Chelyabinsk calling itself by the English name 'Bad Boys' has circulated an underground tape with lyrics that run 'kill all the commies and Komsomol too'.[69] Letters have appeared in Moscow papers from defiant young gangs who openly call themselves Nazis, confident that in the Soviet Union that is the ultimate obscenity to shock their elders.[70]

Of course, as with Western anarchistic-rebellious rock groups like the Sex Pistols, Iron Maiden and Black Sabbath, the intention is probably more to shock and draw attention to themselves than actively to propagate fascist ideology. Komsomol Secretary Victor Mironenko is surely near the mark when he says,

> I think some youngsters have a simplistic reaction to demagogy and violations of social justice, to red tape and the failure of the older generation to match their deeds to words. The immature mind starts looking for an alternative, even resorting to mysticism or the

ugliest ideological systems, such as Nazism. The quest is for an idol, while the Nazi ideology remains alien to them.[71]

As Mironenko admits, it is the unrelenting moralising, the hypocrisy, the double standards, the rigid monopoly of the mass media that have not only produced apathy among many young people, they have pushed some to extremes: the 'if *Pravda*'s for it, I'm against it' syndrome. A British correspondent talks of sitting 'in a Moscow cinema to watch "Battle for Moscow" and [I have] heard the teenagers cheer every time Hitler appears on screen'.[72]

Reports in the Soviet press talk of clean-cut young people dressed in Nazi-imitation uniform: black shirts, jackboots, black glasses and often sporting home-made swastikas. They celebrate Hitler's birthday on 20 April each year, as a *samizdat* source indicates, by demonstrations at the Moscow Pushkin Memorial (since 1982), marches round courtyards and streets punctuated by shouts of 'Heil Hitler' and 'Sieg Heil'; others have burst into youth cafes and discos chanting the same Nazi slogans; and yet others have staged night parades, some even beating up medal-bearing war veterans.[73]

Many of the Nazi thugs seem to be students, especially from the *PTU* technical colleges. *Leningradskaya pravda* has mentioned a Nazi group at *PTU* No. 24 in the city. It not only had its own 'Führer', but sections of SS and SA as well. The thirty-nine-strong group of thirty-seven men and two women wore Nazi uniforms, home-made medals and orders, and had as their stated objective the establishment of National Socialism in the USSR. The newspaper reported that, when questioned, however, the group had no real idea of Nazi ideology. They had never read any Nazi literature.[74]

Other sources talk of support for Nazi ideas from the 'golden youth', the scions of privileged Party, state and army officers.[75] One report mentions the existence of 'quite a few fascist organisations whose members meet in several Moscow cafes. They bear Hitler badges under their jackets and sometimes wear black uniforms.'[76] School heads and Party secretaries are said to have given warnings about possible demonstrations by 'fascistised elements from among non-politically aware groups of young people'.[77] And the Komsomol theoretical journal, *Molodoi kommunist*, has written of 'instances of the penetration of neofascist influences among young people', and 'black shirt extremists in the Western Ukraine and the Baltic area.'[78]

The extreme right has reared its ugly head in a number of newly-formed and already existing organisations, like *Pamyat* (Heritage),

Rodina (Homeland), *Veche* (Popular Assembly in medieval Russian towns) and the Society for the Protection of Historical and Cultural Monuments. All have exhibited quite explicit neofascist, Slavophile symbols and ideology. *Pamyat*, for example, staged a public demonstration in the heart of Moscow in early May 1987, marching on the City Council and demanding a meeting with Boris Yeltsin, the then Moscow Party Secretary. This was followed by public meetings 'at which many young people were present'. The daily *Komsomolskaya pravda* ran an expose that condemned the strident, naked anti-semitism, mystic chauvinism and conspiracy (Jews and Freemasons) theory of *Pamyat*.[79] As a British eyewitness of one *Pamyat* meeting (and himself author of a book on British neofascists) wrote, 'I felt myself carried back in time to those National Front rallies in Britain ten years ago.'[80] And, as he concluded, 'the Gorbachov reforms are coming up against that age-old problem, that freedom of speech means freedom for the extremist as well as the liberal. Lifting the stones from Soviet society is allowing some unpleasant things to crawl out.'[81]

Reports of such right-wing groups have come in from such disparate cities as Novosibirsk, Sverdlovsk, Moscow and Leningrad, and mention a wide-ranging membership, from Party members and high-ranking army officers to scientists and students.[82] Of late they appear to have taken root in a number of the temperance clubs formed during the campaign against drunkenness that was launched in 1985–86.[83] Such is the threat that *Pravda* has warned that action may be taken against 'informal associations' that include 'scoundrels and demagogues who, under the flag of ultra-patriotism, make chauvinistic and anti-semitic sermons'.[84]

SOME CONCLUSIONS

1.   The conservative reaction to radical expressions of youth culture, particularly that imitating Western forms, has its roots, *inter alia*, in the tenacity of Slav and Islamic traditions, in the historical isolation from and suspicion of the West and in the proximity of peasant society. It has to be remembered that on the eve of the Second World War, two-thirds of the Soviet population lived on the land. When Khrushchov fell from power in October 1964, half the population was still rural. Today, two-thirds are urban dwellers. A process that took two and a half centuries in Britain has been crammed into some forty

Soviet years. Even today, as many as 40 per cent of young industrial workers were born in the countryside.[85]

The flight from the land, the desperate urban overcrowding and the crash programme of industrialisation effectively turned a land of peasants (liberated from serfdom only just over a century ago) into an industrial working class. It is hardly surprising, then, that the stresses and strains of modernisation have produced a polarisation of attitudes, first between the generations, and second among young and old alike. The eminent Soviet historian Igor Bestuzhev-Lada has explained that,

> We are today feeling the effects of mass transition from a traditio-
> nal rural to a modern urban way of life. Effectively, before our very
> eyes, we see the disintegration of the old type of family, age-old
> traditions, mores and customs. Young people used to have clear-cut
> and definite duties and life goals – to help the aged and bring up the
> very young.[86] Nothing is clear-cut for young people any more.

2. The areas with the highest crime rates, drug abuse, teenage vandalism, broken marriages (one out of two) are not the major cities, but the medium-sized 'smokestack' cities like Sverdlovsk, Chelyabinsk, Gorky, Vologda, Kurgan and the metropolitan suburbs like Lyubertsy (population 300 000, of whom 80 per cent work in industry[87]). Not only do these areas lack modern amenities and entertainment, have poor public housing and shopping facilities, they are experiencing the withering of the old industries and the retraining of an obsolescent workforce – similar to the problems confronting the depressed industrial northern cities of Britain (minus the unemployment). In fact, the only regions of the USSR that witnessed a net population decline in the 1970s and early 1980s were those in a great swathe around Moscow, with youth the major emigrant.[88]

Both local and central papers are full of cries of despair, of boredom, of envy for the great cities from such decaying suburbs and medium-sized towns. One Soviet journalist likens such places to 'giant railway waiting rooms'.[89] The disoriented young people who remain, envious of the 'city slickers', seem to seek out scapegoats for their plight and deprivation, taking blind revenge on those who flaunt their conspicuous consumption and possess the cherished *propiska* (residential permit) to live in the big cities.

3. In the last two decades Soviet urban society has moved from the six- to the five-day week and entered a phase of relative affluence and leisure; this has given young people new diversions, new aspirations,

new forms of emotional investment that conflict with the old single-minded focus on self-sacrifice and future orientation. Very often the new aspirations have outstripped what the authorities have made or been prepared to make available in the way of leisure activities or youth clubs outside the old-fashioned and sometimes suffocating tutelage of the Komsomol.

Some young people have reacted, particularly in the more liberal but disorienting atmosphere of the Gorbachov reforms, by embracing Western youth culture with all the naive zest that their peers in other modernising societies round the globe have shown towards US 'cultural exports'.

4.   The new liberalisation has created legal opportunities for the extreme right as well as for liberals. The strategy of the new right is to use these legal opportunities to combat liberalisation itself, just as the Black Hundreds and other racist groups did in the 1905 Revolution. As Boris Kagarlitsky has put it,

> The inevitable difficulties and contradictions of the process of change, the unsuccessful economic experiments, the costs of reform – all can be exploited by the reactionary groups in the hope that the course of events will inexorably bring the country to a 'critical point', when the 'restoration of order' and 'normalisation' will become the slogans of the day.[90]

Although life has changed radically since the Stalin years, there exists a certain nostalgia for the past, for a strong master, for a mixture of patriarchal nationalism and totalitarian traditions. And this hankering after the 'old' values is by no means confined to the older generation. The psychological basis for the Lyubery, for example, is a certain nostalgia for Stalinism. As the editor of *Smena* has put it, they 'wish to model their "behaviour" on the most distressing period of our history'.[91]

Erich Fromm once wrote of the 'escape from freedom' whereby certain social groups in society see in democracy a threat to their set traditions, their way of life and security. And this applies not only to adults and the privileged, but to young people and part of the lower orders as well. There appear to be elements of this process at work in Soviet society today, especially with the groups examined in this chapter.

5.   Finally, a major implication for Western theorists of Soviet society in regard to the 'youth revolution' of the last few years is that they will have to rethink their fundamental assumptions about the

Soviet system. They will have to abandon the 'directed society' model that postulates a passive society dominated by an elite and replace it by one that encompasses the active and unofficial youth involvement in changing society.[92]

For what we have been witnessing in the USSR for a period that pre-dates Gorbachov's assumption of power by at least ten years is young people taking affairs into their own hands and operating outside the framework of state institutions. It is a situation that has some similarity with the 'dual power' interregnum between February and October 1917. It is not the elite (Party and Komsomol) that has precipitated reform; it has merely acquiesced in a situation that had existed for several years and was rapidly getting out of official control. While the coming of a new leader has certainly accelerated the process of change, it is youthful opposition to the old regime and mounting disaffection from official institutions and values that have initiated and carried it forward. Where it is heading and which youth group will prevail is impossible to predict. But that, then, is the uncertainty of the struggle to introduce democracy.

Notes

1. Yakovlev, Vladimir, 'Kontora "Lyuberov" ', *Ogonyok*, January 1987, no. 5, p. 20.
2. Protsenko, Alexander, 'Dve versii odnovo proisshestviya', *Molodoi kommunist*, 1986, no. 10, p. 47.
3. Matizen, V., 'Ot otchayaniya k nadezhde', *Iskusstvo kino*, 1987, no. 4, p. 37.
4. Gorbachov, M. S., *Dokumenty i materialy XX syezda VLKSM* (Moscow: Molodaya gvardia, 1987), p. 25.
5. See *Pravda*, 21 December 1987, p. 3.
6. See, for example: Kuklin, Andrei, 'Zona riska,' *Sobesednik*, November 1987, no. 46, p. 13 (about Kazan, where ten teenagers were killed in three years).
7. Walker, Christopher, 'Sinister sons of the revolution', *Times*, 23 March 1987, p. 10.
8. Gorbachov, M. S., 'Doklad no plenume TsK KPSS: O perestroike i kadrovoi politike partii', *Izvestiya*, 28 January 1987, p. 2.
9. Radov, Alexander, 'Deti detochkina', *Komsomolskaya pravda*, 17 October 1986, p. 2.
10. Ibid.
11. Ibid.
12. Ibid.

13. Yakovlev, 'Kontora . . .' (note 1), p. 20.
14. Ibid., p. 21.
15. Sergei, R., 'A nas boitsya . . .' *Komsomolskaya pravda*, 14 December 1986, p. 2.
16. Nosov, Oleg, 'Okh, uzh eti "lyubery"!' *Vecherny Leningrad*, 21 March 1987, p. 3.
17. Yakovlev, 'Kontora . . .' (note 1), p. 20.
18. Shchekochikhin, Yuri, 'Allo, my vas slyshim!' *Literaturnaya gazeta*, 8 April 1987, p. 15.
19. Sergei, R., 'A nas boitsya . . .' (note 15).
20. Shchekochikhin, 'Allo . . .' (note 18).
21. Yakovlev, 'Kontora . . .' (note 1), p. 21.
22. Sergei, R., 'A nas boitsya . . .' (note 15).
23. Yakovlev, 'Kontora . . .' (note 1), p. 20.
24. Ibid.
25. Ibid.
26. Shchekochikhin, 'Allo . . .' (note 18).
27. Ibid.
28. Yakovlev, 'Kontora . . .' (note 1), p. 21.
29. Shchekochikhin, 'Allo . . .' (note 18).
30. Ibid.
31. Ibid.
32. Ibid.
33. 'Moscow youth march against "Lyubery" gangs', *Soviet Weekly*, 7 March 1987, p. 7.
34. Nosov, 'Okh, uzh eti "lyubery"!' (note 16).
35. Yakovlev, 'Kontora . . .' (note 1).
36. Ibid.
37. Shchekochikhin, Yuri, 'O "lyuberakh", i ne tolko o nikh', *Literaturnaya gazeta*, 11 March 1987, p. 1.
38. Shchekochikhin, Yuri, *Literaturnaya gazeta*, 8 April 1987, p. 15.
39. Ibid.
40. Ibid.
41. Smirnova, I., 'Skolko stoit moda?' *Sovetskaya kultura*, 9 April 1986, p. 3.
42. Yakovlev, 'Kontora . . .' (note 1).
43. Ibid.
44. Pavlova-Silvanskaya, M., 'Impatience', *Soviet Weekly*, 13 June 1987, p. 5.
45. Tursunov, Valeri, 'A newspaper and a friend', in *Soviet Weekly*, 28 November 1987, p. 15 (reprinted from *Moskovsky komsomolets*, 5 September 1987).
46. Kagarlitsky, Boris, 'The intelligentsia and the changes', *New Left Review*, July/August 1987, no. 164, p. 22.
47. Korolkov, Igor, 'Iz boya ne vyshli', *Sobesednik*, February 1987, no. 6, p. 5.
48. Chernyak, Igor, 'Ne iskat po zemle zhizni sladkoi', *Sobesednik*, December 1987, no. 49, p. 4.
49. Matizen (see note 3).

50. Zverev, Alexander, 'Opalyonnaya sovest', *Sobesednik*, April 1987, no. 17, p. 15.
51. Ibid.
52. Korolkov, 'Iz boya ...' (note 47). See also Serazhetdinov, Marat, 'Khochetsya v nebo', *Molodoi kommunist*, May 1987, no. 5, p. 68.
53. Kozin, V., 'Kaskad speshit na pomoshch,' *Komsomolskaya pravda*, 20 January 1987, p. 2.
54. Shchekochikhin (see note 37).
55. Vishnevsky, B., '"Koroli" trubyat sbor', *Komsomolskaya pravda*, 22 April 1987, p. 2.
56. Gurvich, Dina, 'Nabolelo', *Smena*, October 1986, no. 20, p. 8.
57. Kolinichenko, Vladimir, 'Pochemu na komsomolskuyu rabotu ne vydvigayt byvshikh voinov-internatsionalistov?' *Sobesednik*, May 1987, no. 22, p. 3.
58. Zhilnikov, Leonid, 'Dlya nas nyet "tyla"', *Sobesednik*, January 1987, no. 5, p. 2.
59. Muratov, Dmitri, and Sorokin, Yuri, 'Dublyor vykhodit na svyaz', *Sobesednik*, March 1987, no. 13, pp. 8–9.
60. Tsagolova, L., 'Muzhskoi razgovor', *Sobesednik*, November 1987, no. 47, p. 2.
61. Ibid.
62. Chernyak, 'Ne iskat ...' (note 48).
63. Ibid.
64. Ibid.
65. Ibid.
66. Goncharenko, V., 'Budut plastinki', *Sobesednik*, November 1987, no. 48, p. 11.
67. 'Shalunushki i predatelstvo', *Sobesednik*, May 1986, no. 21, p. 6.
68. 'Prigovor i "advokaty"', *Sobesednik*, June 1986, no. 26, p. 6.
69. See Walker, Martin, 'The desperate pain in the heart of Russia', *Guardian*, 29 December 1986, p. 18.
70. Ibid.
71. See 'It Isn't Easy to be Young?' *Soviet Weekly*, 6 June 1987, p. 12.
72. Walker, 'Sinister Sons ...' (note 7).
73. See 'Fashizm v SSSR', *Strana i mir* (Munich), 1984, nos 1–2, p. 51; 'Organizatsiya yunykh fashistov', *Strana i mir*, 1985, no. 5, p. 18; 'Ne tolko v Azii', *Strana i mir*, 1986, no. 12, pp. 10–11.
74. Koshvanets, V., 'Standartenfuerer ot Maloi Okhty,' *Leningradskaya pravda*, 11 July 1987, p. 3. Within the space of three months, May–August 1987, articles on young fascists appeared in several periodicals, including *Smena, Moskovsky komsomolets, Leningradskaya pravda* and *Molodyozh Estonii*.
75. 'Organizatsiya yunykh fashistov', *Strana i mir*, 1985, no. 5, p. 18.
76. Ibid.
77. Ibid.
78. Bocharova, V., 'Nazyvat veshchi svoimi imenami', *Molodoi kommunist*, 1987, no. 7, p. 78; Palamarchuk, O., 'Protiv chevo my boremsya?' *Molodoi kommunist*, 1988, no. 3, p. 93.

79.   Losoto, Y., 'V bespamyatstve', *Komsomolskaya pravda*, 22 May 1987, p. 4.
80.   Walker, Martin, 'A nasty sight in a Soviet', *Guardian*, 25 May 1987, p. 11.
81.   Ibid.
82.   Klyuyev, Vladimir, 'My redko sovershayem smelye postupki', *Sobesednik*, August 1987, no. 32, p. 5.
83.   Kagarlitsky, 'The intelligentsia . . .' (note 46), p. 22.
84.   See *Pravda*, 27 December 1987, p. 2.
85.   Sandrigailo, V. L., *Politika i molodyozh* (Minsk: Nauka i tekhnika, 1986) p. 19.
86.   Bestuzhev-Lada, Igor, quoted in Kuklin, 'Zona riska', *Sobesednik*, November 1987, no. 46, p. 13.
87.   'Lyubertsy – pri svete fonarei', *Sobesednik*, February 1987, no. 7, pp. 10–15.
88.   Walker, Martin, 'All dressed up but with nowhere to go', *Guardian*, 30 December 1986, p. 17.
89.   Yanbukhtin, Renat, 'Arifmetika i algebra aktivnosti', *Molodoi kommunist*, 1987, no. 5, p. 11.
90.   Kagarlitsky, 'The intelligentsia . . .' (note 46), p. 22.
91.   Likhanov, A., *Knizhnoye obozrenie*, 1987, no. 9.
92.   The same applies to the 'totalitarian', 'administered society', 'ideological system' and even the more participatory 'institutional pluralism' models.

Name Index

Subject Index